LIBERATE
YOUR BUSINESS

BECKY MOLLENKAMP

Dedication

To Terry and Gus. You make my world brighter, and I couldn't have reached this goal without your love and support. I love you the most! I win.

Contents

Contents

Introduction

Business Is Broken

The "American Dream" teaches us that success is available to anyone who's willing to work hard enough. In entrepreneurship, that belief shows up as a set of quiet rules: never stop building and optimizing, always be selling, your work is your worth, and treat exhaustion as proof of doing it right.

Over the last two decades, the rise of online business wrapped the myth of meritocracy in new technology, promising to make entrepreneurship more accessible. "All you need is an idea, an internet connection, and effort." But the internet just optimized capitalist extraction. It's the same rules on a larger scale.

In 2020, the world shut down and millions of people were pushed online at once. Online business became saturated as more people chased the false promise of "passive income." The only people who actually got rich, though, were those teaching others how to get rich (often following some version of the same formula: churn out endless free content, lure people onto your email list, and pressure them into buying). By 2022, the noise became deafening and attention thinned. The "tried-and-true" tactics of the previous decade stopped working, not because individuals did anything wrong, but because systems built on endless growth *always* fail. And now people are scrambling for the next tactic or platform that will fix everything.

All of this has unfolded against a backdrop of a broader political reckoning. Donald Trump didn't invent capitalism, hate, inequity, authoritarianism, and colonialism. But he has exposed how many people with privilege mistook insulation from harm for moral superiority (allowing them to believe that those who struggle just haven't worked as hard as them). For many, the current climate is disorienting and painful. For others, it's merely an amplification of the harm that's always been part of their lives and their ancestry.

For entrepreneurs who care about social justice, the question isn't "how do I make this work?" It's, "what's this costing, and how do I not cause harm?"

The way we've been taught to do business is breaking people. Productivity has risen year after year. Meanwhile, employee engagement, well-being, and job satisfaction have been declining for decades, with a major nosedive since 2020. CEOs have gone from earning an average of 20 times more than their workers in the 1960s to nearly 300 times more today without a comparable increase in worker pay. A small group of executives, shareholders, and investors reap the rewards, while the people doing the actual labor struggle to make ends meet.

The widening inequality isn't only economic; it's also psychological. It trains us to see survival as a personal achievement instead of a collective responsibility. It rewards competition and hoarding, punishes care and collaboration, and blames individuals when the system inevitably grinds them down. Capitalism requires a permanent underclass to function, and the myth of upward mobility keeps people compliant. We're not in a "tough period." The system is doing exactly what it was designed to do.

Everything from time to relationships becomes a metric to be measured. Structural harm is turned into personal failure: "fix your mindset," "manage your time better," "be more disciplined." The result is a constant sense of inadequacy, even when you're doing everything "right." It's why every decision feels urgent, every pause risky, and every boundary a liability. The pressure doesn't stay in your head. It settles into your body in the form of tight shoulders, shallow breathing, a pit in your stomach, trouble sleeping, and worse. When a system treats your capacity as infinite, your nervous system pays the price.

Inequity and burnout are the conditions that keep the system running. Capitalism only works if people feel behind, pressured, and replaceable. When you're scrambling just to keep up and survive, you don't have the time or energy to question the rules. When harm is individualized, people turn their frustration inward instead of toward the structures extracting from them. Those with power profit by selling "solutions" to fix what the system keeps breaking. That's why the answers we're offered are almost always personal. But no amount of self-improvement can solve a structural problem. You can't "mindset" your way out of racism and sexism. Once you see this, the question shifts from "what's wrong with me?" to "what can we do differently?"

It's also important to recognize that while the system harms everyone, it's not equally distributed. Women, 2SLGBTQIA+ people, disabled people, and most especially Black, Brown, and Indigenous people are expected to absorb more labor and risk, while being told to feel grateful for even having access at all. The more of those identities you hold, the greater your exposure to harm.

Values-driven entrepreneurs are caught in a double bind. If you follow the rules, you betray your values. If you break them, you risk your livelihood. You desperately want to be ethical, authentic, and human, but you're also worried about the cost of living, paying salaries, and reaching profit goals. It's tiring.

Business itself isn't the enemy, but the capitalist rules we've been given are neither neutral nor inevitable. They must be questioned and unlearned. They must also be redesigned, which starts with changing how decisions get made, and what we're willing to sacrifice to make them.

For a long time, I thought the answer was to try harder, manage better, and be more disciplined. Eventually, I took inspiration from Maya Angelou's *I Know Why the Caged Bird Sings*, and started asking a new question. What if the problem isn't the bird? What if the problem is the cage? We can spend our lives perfecting ourselves inside the cage of a system that was designed to deny us freedom, or we can start asking how to open the cage door.

You don't need another hack, three-step plan, or morning routine to solve your problems. What you need is permission to stop contorting your humanity to fit a system that was never built with your flourishing in mind. Liberation begins when "survival" or "more" stop being the sole measures of success.

Liberate Your Business isn't anti-work, anti-ambition, or anti-earning. It's anti-extraction. It challenges the version of business shaped by white-supremacist capitalist patriarchy, one that treats people as expenses and burnout as a cost of success. This book invites you to interrogate the rules you've been given, and to unlearn the beliefs that keep you trapped inside cycles of urgency, scarcity, and self-sacrifice. The goal is to choose what "enough" looks like for you.

I've written this book for entrepreneurs, founders, and leaders who want their work to reflect their values, and who are tired of being told that the only way to succeed is to override their bodies, communities, or ethics.

Capitalism would have you believe that business liberation is impossible. In reality, it's already being practiced. Black, Indigenous, disabled, and queer communities have been building survival economies, mutual aid networks, cooperative care, and relationship-based leadership for generations out of necessity. These models weren't trends, they were built to keep people alive and connected under hostile conditions.

Much of what we now call "values-led" business draws from wisdom forged by abolitionist thinkers who taught us to imagine beyond control and punishment. By disability justice activists who insisted that interdependence, pace, and access are strengths. By Black scholars who told us to see who does labor vs. who gets credit. By Indigenous teachers who remind us that reciprocity is a natural way of life. This book is in conversation with those lineages.

The question isn't whether another way exists, but whether we're willing to stop treating dominant business culture as the default and to begin tolerating the discomfort of doing things differently.

The world we're building is one where businesses are designed around real human limits, where growth is a choice, and where success is measured by sustainability, care, and whether work actually supports the lives of the people doing it. A world where business decisions are made with context. Pace and consent matter. Interdependence is a strength. Where business is done in ways that reduce harm, expand choice, and make it possible to keep going without disappearing in the process.

What follows is not a blueprint for winning capitalism. It's a guide for refusing what no longer works and practicing something else instead. Something slower, more honest, and rooted in dignity and collective thriving. This book offers language for what you've been feeling, frameworks for understanding how power operates in business, and practices for designing work that doesn't require you to disappear to succeed. It won't tell you what to build. It will help you decide what's worth building, and what you're done sacrificing to get there. The shift won't be instant or perfect, but it will be tangible. It starts with how you relate to your work and yourself.

Think of this book as a companion, not a command. It's a reminder of your humanness inside a system that profits when you forget it. It won't ask you to fake certainty or move faster than your capacity allows. It will invite you to question what you've been told is normal and correct, and to experiment with ways of working that make room for your full self.

You don't need to fix yourself to belong. You already do.

How to Use This Book

You'll move through this book in the same order that liberation tends to move through us. First internally, then relationally, then structurally, and finally toward the new world we're choosing to build.

Section 1: Internalized Systems names the air we've been breathing. We'll look at how mindset culture hides systemic harm, how shame and body politics distort our sense of worth, how risk gets unevenly distributed, and how perfectionism is a myth that frames our struggles as personal failures instead of predictable outcomes of the systems we live inside.

Section 2: Unlearning the Money-Work-Worth Connection asks you to zoom out. We'll unspool the lies about income and status, the weaponizing of relationships, the cult of productivity, and how time is used against us, the attention economy is designed to distract us, and the pressure to monetize every corner of our lives depletes us. It's a deep exhale and an opportunity to say, "Oh, it was never me. It was always the system."

Section 3: The Business We're Told to Build takes aim at the machinery. We dismantle funnels, algorithms, authenticity theater, the credibility game, the invisible labor load on marginalized founders, and the extractive nature of team building. We expose how traditional entrepreneurship quietly recreates empire, and how easily we end up reinforcing the conditions we're trying to escape.

And finally, in **Section 4: The Future We Can Choose**, we explore the compass of True North, the strategic power of boundaries, the revolutionary role of pleasure, the necessity of collaboration, the responsibility of activism, the practice of accountability, and the invitation to build a liberated legacy.

This book is not meant to be read in one sitting, but to be lived with over time. Each section builds on the one before it, guiding you from awareness to unlearning, from unlearning to disruption, from disruption to reimagining, and finally from reimagining to practice.

Each chapter follows a rhythm so you're not dropped in without support:

- **Reality Check:** Names the lie capitalism told you.
- **Journaling Pause:** Helps you integrate ideas, not just think about them.
- **Liberatory Reframe:** Offers a new lens rooted in anti-capitalist values.
- **Micro Liberations:** Gives you tangible practices to start right away.

You can read straight through, or jump to a chapter where curiosity feels most alive. Your intuition knows what you need most, so trust it. Mark up and dog-ear the pages. Write in the margins. Let it be messy. Talk about it with your team, clients, and friends. This work grows in community and conversation. And you don't have to agree with everything in these pages to benefit from the book. Take what resonates, leave what doesn't, and stay curious about what your resistance may be protecting. Most importantly, don't rush.

Capitalism teaches us to move fast, and this book challenges you to slow down and make choices from a place of dignity.

My Lens

I'm a white, middle-class, and educated person living in the United States. I use she/they pronouns, but am perceived as cisgender. I'm pansexual in a hetero marriage. I'm a mother, business owner, and someone who benefits daily from systems of privilege. Those identities give me access and blind spots. I do my best to name the limits of my perspective rather than pretend they don't exist. When I reference ideas born from communities I don't belong to, I do so as a student and a witness, not as an authority.

My fingerprints are all over this work, but you'll also see the traces of everyone who has helped in my unlearning and re-education processes. This book is not just mine. It's part of a larger conversation happening among feminist and womanist thinkers, organizers, and entrepreneurs around the world who are trying to imagine freer ways to live and work.

As a coach and community builder, I've seen far too many brilliant people measure their worth in revenue or reach, even when those metrics betray their values. I wrote this book to provide an easy-to-follow framework for running a business that honors your ambition *and* your humanity.

Paying Tribute to My Teachers

In the early 2010s, I became deeply interested in understanding the oppressive systems that helped to inform my feelings of unworthiness. As is common for white women like myself, that work began by learning about patriarchy.

Then in 2014, a police officer murdered teenager Michael Brown less than a mile from my home. That event changed my life's trajectory. I expanded my unlearning when I read about intersectionality. Coined by law professor and civil rights advocate Kimberlé Crenshaw in 1989, the word recognizes that identities don't exist independently but intersect, and the overlap compounds oppression.

My first and most important teacher was bell hooks, starting with her *Feminism is for Everybody* and then, most importantly, *All About Love*. But my worldview has continued to expand thanks to many teachers and friends. The lineage that

informs my own liberation, as well as much of this work, includes: Audre
Lorde, Angela Y Davis, Gloria Steinem, adrienne maree brown, Robin Wall
Kimmerer, Tricia Hersey, Sonya Renee Taylor, Feminista Jones, Mariame Kaba,
Mia Birdsong, Rachel Cargle, Resmaa Menakem, Deepa Iyer, Ericka Hart, Koa
Beck, Desireé B. Stephens, Nikki Blak, Portia Burch, Imani Barbarin, Alok
Vaid-Menon, Toi Smith, Kelly Diels, Taina Brown, Faith Clarke, Jordan Maney,
CV Harquail, and so many more. They have shown me that liberation is not
theory, it's a practice. I stand on their shoulders with deep gratitude and a
commitment to carrying their lessons forward with integrity.

AI Statement

I used generative AI in the creation of this book, primarily to review and
organize content I'd previously created for my blog and podcasts. AI helped
me determine what was a good fit for the book and to outline the content. The
words are all my own. As a neurodiverse person, organizing a decade's worth
of content may never have been accessible to me without AI assistance.

That said, AI is not neutral. It consumes enormous amounts of energy, is
built on the often invisible labor of underpaid and exploited workers, and
causes real harm to people and the planet. As with other oppressive systems,
these harms fall heaviest on those with the most marginalized identities.

We can't opt out of the flawed systems that we're forced to operate within.
All we can do is make conscious choices, reduce harm when possible, and take
responsibility for the tradeoffs we make. Liberation cares more about
transparency, mutual care, and accountability than perfection (an impossible
standard). This book was written by a human, shaped by community, and
supported (deliberately and sparingly) by tools that made the work possible.

I purchased renewable energy credits through Terrapass that more than
offset the electricity I used during this project. This doesn't solve the problem
(there is no ethical consumption under capitalism), but it's one way I attempt to
reduce harm and to take responsibility for the impact of my choices.

A Note on Readiness

The hardest part of reading this book may not be realizing that you're in a cage. It may be realizing the door has been open longer than you thought, and you're still not ready to step out.

The cage is familiar. It has kept you fed, safe, praised, and employed. Outside the cage is uncertain, unstructured, and full of risks you don't yet know how to survive (or risks that you *cannot* survive, which is a very real possibility depending on the marginalized identities you hold).

Liberation isn't proven by leaving. It may instead look like staying inside the cage on purpose while you gather strength, learn what your wings can do, and decide (on your own timeline) when and how to move. It may even mean never leaving because to do so would be harmful, and instead finding ways to remain inside with greater support. And that's okay, friend.

Section 1

Internalized Systems

Most business books jump straight to tactics, but the systems you live inside have shaped you long before you set prices or devise a marketing plan. When those beliefs are formed by white-supremacist capitalist patriarchy, even the most well-intentioned strategies can reproduce harm.

You've absorbed judgments about what makes you worthy, how much rest you're allowed, and what it costs to belong. Over time, those ideas start to feel like your own. That's why this book starts here, naming the systems that built those beliefs.

These chapters will help loosen the grip of internalized capitalism so you can actually take in the rest of the book. You'll see how "mindset" became a weapon, how shame disconnects you from intuition, how perfectionism is a system rather than a personality flaw, and how fear, risk, and scarcity were deliberately engineered to keep people compliant. Once you can see how deeply you've been conditioned, you can stop trying to fix yourself and start questioning the rules you were given.

This is the foundation. Without it, any strategy is likely to quietly reinforce old, toxic rules. This is the end of the self-blame era, and the beginning of building better, more liberatory businesses.

1.

Is It Really Mindset?

Wanting change and trusting yourself enough to choose it are not the same thing. When trust in our own judgment breaks down, we're conditioned to look inward for the problem. This book starts with mindset because capitalism is effective at disguising itself as personal failure.

Before I understood liberation, I called myself a mindset coach. Like many white women coaches, I believed that mindset is the key to everything. I repeated phrases that now make me cringe: "Is it a limiting belief?" "Where are you playing small?" "What would you do if you weren't afraid?" At the time, I believed "change your thoughts, change your life" worked. I said things like that to clients navigating trauma, to a trans client trying to survive in a violent world, to Black women living in a racist system. What they needed was material support, not a privileged white woman reframing oppression as a "mindset problem." I wasn't malicious, but I was unaware of the harm I was replicating.

Only after a few years of unpacking white-supremacist capitalist patriarchy did I realize that I hadn't yet extended the same unlearning to my coaching work. I came to see that I could learn more from Black feminists about coaching than from anyone in the traditional self-help machine. Over time, I understood my job wasn't to teach people to think better, and the idea that I could empower anyone meant I believed power was mine to give. I had to decolonize the tools I used, examine the power dynamics in my client relationships, shift from individualist narratives to collective ones, and learn how to be in space with people whose lives differ from mine. Mindset work wasn't the problem; the problem was when it didn't include naming systems, getting consent, understanding trauma-awareness, or analyzing power.

This chapter is an invitation to interrogate the system instead of yourself. You'll learn how to recognize when mindset language is quietly asking for your consent to harm, and how to withhold that consent without turning it inward.

Mindset, Capitalist Style

The business world leans heavily on frameworks borrowed from cognitive behavioral therapy (CBT), a model meant to help people change unhelpful thoughts and behaviors. It was developed by white men and, like all frameworks created inside dominant culture, it carries their blind spots. In business spaces, it's often stripped of therapeutic context and delivered as universal truth.

You've probably heard CBT framed as "circumstances are neutral, but how you think about them is what you can control." But the reality is that business exists inside systems shaped by oppression, and those conditions aren't neutral.

Entrepreneurs learn this framework from coaches and experts who typically aren't trained in trauma-informed care, and don't ask: "Whose reality does this model assume? Who does it work for, and who does it fail?" Treating structural violence as a mindset issue puts responsibility where it doesn't belong. Personal growth can't substitute for collective accountability.

Liberatory thinkers show us another way. Trudi Lebron calls out how white-dominant coaching turns strategies for surviving systemic harm into personal failings. Erica Courdae says frameworks reproduce their creators' worldview and can't be neutral. Telling business owners to change their mindset about racism at work, medical trauma, financial strain, disability, or safety issues is erasure.

It's not an accident that mindset messaging exploded as the online business world became saturated with white women selling personal transformation as a shortcut to success. "Your results are your responsibility" pairs neatly with "Success is proof of your worth." If you're struggling, they say, it's because you didn't believe hard enough. In fact, it's because you're building a business inside systems that were never designed for your safety, dignity, or thriving.

Mindset *can* be helpful, but not when it's used to bypass lived reality.

<table>
<tr><td rowspan="4">journal
your
journey</td><td>When has mindset advice made me feel smaller?</td></tr>
<tr><td>Have I mistaken survival strategies for personal flaws?</td></tr>
<tr><td>Who benefits when I blame myself for systemic failures?</td></tr>
<tr><td>What mindset messages shaped how I run my business?</td></tr>
</table>

Consciousness Without Cruelty

At its best, "mindset" work looks like Dr. Barbara J. Love's Liberatory Consciousness social justice framework, which helped inform my coaching model (below), a feminist reimagining of Cognitive Behavioral Therapy.

1. Context: Nothing is neutral, so name the privilege, oppression, and trauma at play. What's happening *to* you matters as much as what's happening *in* you.

2. Compassion: Your thoughts are shaped by lived experience, not personal deficiency. "Negative" feelings like fear, anger, anxiety, or despair aren't "limiting beliefs," they're information (and often reflect a truth, such as your very real need for safety, that dominant culture denies).

3. Embodiment: You can't "mindset" your way out of a nervous system response. Let the body complete the stress cycle before deciding what's next.

4. Safety: Pause to take considered action based on your capacity and safety, not what you "should" do.

5. Redefine the Result: Using this approach, you'll arrive at a self-honoring result that protects your humanity (even if that isn't the "best" choice).

If someone's version of mindset work ignores or diminishes your reality, history, or truth, it isn't healing or helpful. And it definitely isn't liberation.

When Mindset Isn't the Problem

Mindset work is the wrong tool when you're dealing with:

- **X** Racism, sexism, ableism, homophobia, transphobia
- **X** Medical, financial, or generational trauma
- **X** Burnout due to overwork or caregiving
- **X** Housing insecurity, disability access, or lack of childcare
- **X** Abusive relationships
- **X** Grief, loss, or major life transitions
- **X** Unsafe workplaces

These are not mindset problems. They're material conditions. You don't think your way out of them. You resource your way through them.

The Wrong (and Better) Questions

System-shaped questions	Liberatory questions
"What's wrong with me?"	"What happened to me?"
"Why can't I change?"	"Who benefits when I blame myself?"
"How do I stop feeling this way?"	"What do I need to feel safe?"
"How do I improve this problem?"	"What help would make this easier?"
"Why can't I get over this?"	"What if this is trying to protect me?"
"Why aren't I more confident?"	"How could it be safe to take up space?"
"Why am I struggling with this?"	"What support isn't accessible to me?"
"Why am I not further along?"	"What timeline am I measuring against?"
"Why am I always the problem?"	"Who made me believe that?"

Real risk is anything that costs your humanity. Real safety is built together.

You can't mindset your way out of oppression.

Micro-Liberations

Try these to undo the conditioning that blames you for systemic problems.

Name the system before naming the thought.
When you catch a self-critical or fear-based thought, pause and say: "This is oppression talking." Only then should you interrogate the thought.

Build a "reality check" circle.
Pick one to three people you can text when you're spiraling. Choose people who will reflect your truth when mindset culture tries to distort it.

Get consent before mindset conversations.
Ask: "Do I have capacity to look at this right now?" If the answer is no, choose a regulating action instead (walk, nap, food, silence).

Don't outsource your truth.
Before seeking advice, ask whether external input will support or override your knowing.

Your body is a source of truth.
When something feels "off," name one physical sensation (tight chest, clenched jaw). Your body registers misalignment before your brain.

Let one feeling be unfixed.
Once a day, let yourself feel something without improving it. Set a 3-5 minute timer and just notice the feeling without reframing, or solving.

Mindset may have its place, but not in explaining away the very real barriers you face, whether that's sexism, racism, ableism, classism, homophobia, anti-fat bias, family responsibilities, neurodiversity, trauma, or any other of the thousand ways capitalism negatively affects lives.

Liberation begins when you stop gaslighting yourself, start trusting your own knowing, and recognize the difference between a limiting belief and an actual limitation that deserves care, accommodation, and rest.

If you do only one thing from this chapter, do this:
Notice where you've been taught to treat systemic harm as a personal flaw.
If a thought comes up that says "this is just my mindset," pause and ask:
"What might be true if this isn't about me at all?"

2.

Shame, Worth, and the Body

I knew my first marriage was dying before my ex-husband did. There wasn't a glaring problem, just a growing distance between us. Instead of saying the words out loud, I swallowed them. I believed that I should be grateful for our good-on-paper life, so I saw my unhappiness as a personal failure.

Rather than thinking "I'm not happy in this marriage," I believed "I am bad for not being happy in this marriage." That is shame and, after years, it became an unbearable weight. In a foolish effort to get the longing for change "out of my system," I had a one-night stand, which only compounded my shame.

Cheating was a terrible choice, but my marriage didn't collapse because of that one decision. Ultimately, it ended because I was only performing the role of "good wife," not showing up as my whole self. A relationship built on performance is fragile, no matter how "perfect" it appears.

White-supremacist capitalist patriarchy had conditioned me to be a "good girl." That meant getting a good education, then a good job, and marrying a good man. I checked the boxes, but I wasn't fulfilled...and I was terrified to tell anyone how I felt. What if people thought I was selfish or ungrateful? I shaped my life around expectations instead of my truth, and was left with the sinking feeling that "I made my bed so I had to lie in it." I minimized my needs until I could no longer hear them.

Only years later could I name what had been happening. At the time, it didn't feel like conditioning. I simply accepted it as a personal failure. I thought that wanting something different meant there was something wrong with me, so I learned to manage my desire instead of trusting it.

Shame is how the system lives inside the body. When people are taught to believe they're the problem, they stop telling the truth (even to themselves) about what they need, want, and know. This chapter is about how shame gets tied to worth, and how the body holds truths the mind is trained to override.

Shame Is a Tool of Control

As Ijeoma Oluo writes in *So You Want to Talk About Race*, white-supremacist capitalist patriarchy is an abusive system built on shame. The pattern:

- The system tells you there's something wrong with who you are.
- You learn to hide those parts to avoid punishment or judgment.
- You start performing acceptability instead of telling the truth.
- You're led to believe you're alone in feeling this way.
- This makes you withdraw, so you don't receive support.
- Eventually, you internalize the message and stop seeking justice or change.
- The cycle continues without anyone needing to enforce it directly.

This is why shame feels intimate even when it's structural. The system doesn't have to police us constantly because we learn to do it to ourselves. Eventually, the cage moves inside the body. At that point, compliance feels like a choice we're making. "[Shame] eats at you until it fully consumes you," wrote Alok Vaid-Menon in *Beyond the Gender Binary*. "Then you cannot tell the difference between their shame and your own."

Shame harms everyone, but it doesn't land the same. For those with marginalized identities, educator Tovi Scruggs-Hussein says, shame is shaped by real consequences for being yourself. It's a reflex to protect yourself from a system that punishes your existence. For those with privilege, especially white people, shame often shows up as defensiveness, fragility, or the urge to be seen as one of "the good ones." It's the overwhelm that comes from complicity in a system you didn't create but from which you nonetheless benefit.

"Shame is actually the underlying emotion of the discomfort that primarily drives fragility," Scruggs-Hussein says. "It keeps those with oppressor identities from creating repair." Whether shame makes you shrink or shut down (or both at different times), it serves the system.

<table>
<tr><td rowspan="4">journal
your
journey</td><td>Whose approval was I trained to chase?</td></tr>
<tr><td>What parts of myself was I made to believe are bad?</td></tr>
<tr><td>How does shame silence my needs?</td></tr>
<tr><td>Who benefits when I stay silent?</td></tr>
</table>

Returning to Right Relation

If shame is the voice of domination inside your body, then liberation is the practice of answering it with love.

"The moment we choose to love, we begin to move against domination, against oppression. The moment we choose to love, we begin to move toward freedom, to act in ways that liberate ourselves and others," wrote bell hooks in *Outlaw Culture: Resisting Representations*. Love isn't softness or sentimentality. It's a disciplined refusal to abandon yourself even when the system trains you to.

What does that look like in real life?

1. Anchor in dignity. When shame says "you are bad," remember the values that guide how you do your work. You're not required to violate your own humanity to prove your own worthiness.

2. Come back to your body. "We heal primarily in and through the body, not just through the rational brain," says Resmaa Menakem in *My Grandmother's Hands*. When shame spikes, place a hand on your chest or take one slow exhale to remind your nervous system that you're safe enough to stay present.

3. Practice relational repair. Shame survives in secrecy. It loosens its grip when witnessed. "All flourishing is mutual," Robin Wall Kimmerer writes in *Braiding Sweetgrass*. Connecting with a trusted person, even briefly, is often enough to interrupt the pattern and bring you back into relationship.

A client with a successful marketing business felt unfulfilled selling to corporate clients. She dreamed of creating a community space where women could show up as their full selves, but charging for it brought shame. Old religious conditioning said "good women" give selflessly. Making money from helping others felt wrong.

Her body told the truth. When she thought about the project, she felt grounded and alive. When she imagined giving it away for free, she felt exhausted. With that information, she explored a middle path—pricing that honored her labor and allowed access for those she most wanted to serve.

The Demonization of Intuition

White-supremacist capitalist patriarchy elevates logic, reason, and rationality as the gold standards of a person's intelligence and worth. But that's not inherently true, nor neutral. It's political.

The system rewards:	It punishes:
People with historic access to formal education (white, male, wealthy, Western).	Embodied knowing (the wisdom of people who had to read the room to survive).
Forms of knowledge that benefit the ruling class (profit, data, productivity, hierarchy).	Intuition in communities who weren't allowed to rely on institutions for safety or justice.
Communication styles of dominant groups (linear, emotionless, individualistic).	Emotion, instinct, relational awareness, or intelligence models it couldn't fully colonize.

Devaluing intuition wasn't an accident. If you teach an entire population to distrust the wisdom of their bodies, you make them easier to control. If you override their knowing, they become easier to exploit. If you make them doubt their own signals, they're more likely to defer to authority.

Shame serves as a mechanism to interrupt intuition by flooding the body with fear and self-doubt, then handing the mic back to the "rational" mind, which mostly repeats whatever the dominant culture said you should believe. So when you feel shame for being "too emotional" or for trusting your gut over your brain, the system is doing exactly what it's designed to do. It desperately needs to disconnect you from the most anti-oppressive intelligence you already hold.

Intuition hasn't gone anywhere. It's still speaking beneath the noise of shame. Reclaiming it is not rejecting intelligence; it's a return to *natural* intelligence. It's a return to yourself, and a rebellion against oppression.

Shame is the system's voice inside your body.
Intuition is your voice trying to break through.

Distinguishing the Voices

Learn the difference among shame, logic, and intuition so you can tell whose voice you're hearing, and choose the one that leads you back to freedom.

Shame
- Internalized judgment from external systems
- Loud, urgent, moralizing ("you're bad")
- Disconnects you from your body
- Reinforces obedience, self-surveillance, and perfectionism
- Shuts down intuition by making you doubt your own signals
- Serves patriarchy, racism, capitalism—not you

Logic/Reason
- Head-based processing
- Useful for planning, analyzing, and sequencing
- Culturally coded as "superior" because it's tied to white, male norms
- Helpful, but incomplete without embodied wisdom
- Becomes oppressive when treated as the only valid way of knowing

Intuition
- Body-based knowing
- Pattern recognition from lived experience
- Quiet, grounded, nonjudgmental
- Rooted in connection and self-trust
- Supports dignity and safety
- Emerges when you slow down and listen

How They Interact
Shame impersonates logic by sounding like "common sense" or "good judgment." Logic can clarify intuition, but can also drown it out if over-relied on. Shame polices you. Logic organizes you. Intuition protects you. When all three are in right relationship, you make decisions rooted in truth, not fear.

Learning to Hear Your Intuition

After a lifetime of allowing shame to suppress your intuition, it can feel impossible to hear it. Have patience. Quieting the conditioning so you can hear your embodied truth takes time, but it's possible.

1. Start with the body. Intuition speaks through sensation before it becomes thoughts or words. Begin to notice your body's signals. Is your chest open or contracted? Are your shoulders lifted or tight? Is your jaw clenched or relaxed? At all times, ask yourself, "does this feel like expansion or contraction?"

2. Track evidence. Write down moments when you knew something before you could explain it (don't worry about whether it led to the "right" result). Are there patterns to how your intuition feels?

3. Use sensory grounding. Intuition is muted when the nervous system is bracing. In those moments, try orienting (naming colors in the room), taking 4 to 6 deep breaths, or placing your hands on your heart or belly. Once your body settles, ask, "what do I already know?"

4. Distinguish between intuition and conditioning. This isn't easy because conditioning wants you to believe it is your truth, not the oppressors'. Slowly learn the difference by asking yourself, "does this feel like my truth, or does it feel like expectation, fear, or anxiety?"

5. Gather data. Intuition is a whisper to consider, not an order to obey. You don't have to act immediately (or even do what it says). Listening is enough, especially when you are just beginning to hear the voice.

6. Slow down responses. Shame is loud, certain, and urgent. Intuition is quiet, grounded, and slow. Delay a default "it's fine," and practice a pause, "let me get back to you." Take a beat to listen for your knowing before responding.

7. Practice tiny truths. Intuition gets louder the more you honor it. Find small ways to begin speaking your truth. "I'm tired." "I'd rather not." "I want Italian for dinner." Truth builds self-trust, which rebuilds intuition.

8. Quiet the noise. Take five minutes a day of silence (no phone or other inputs) to notice what arises in your body. Intuition is far more difficult to hear when it's trying to compete with the noise of daily life.

Micro-Liberations

Small, daily choices to break shame's spell and rebuild trust in yourself.

Practice "shame naming."
When something stings, pause and say, "this is shame talking. Not the truth." Naming it can reduce its power.

Interrupt the spiral.
When you notice looping thoughts, stand up and change rooms. Movement resets more than thinking does.

Shrink the decision.
If a choice feels overwhelming, reduce it to:"what's the least harmful option *right now*?" You don't need the best one, just the least damaging.

Replace *self* with *system* (when accurate).
If a problem shows up repeatedly for people who share your identity, it's structural. You don't need proof; recognizing the pattern is enough.

Share one shame story.
Choose one safe person. Share one small truth. Say upfront, "I don't need advice, just witnessing." Notice what shifts in your body afterward.

Celebrate desire.
Once this week, name a want without explaining, optimizing, or earning it. You can want something because you want it. That's the practice.

Perfection, discipline, and "mindset" won't silence shame, but you can begin to free yourself from its unkind grip by refusing to abandon the parts of you that the system said you need to hide. Every moment you choose curiosity over criticism, intuition over "intelligence," and connection over silence, you are silencing shame and reclaiming your truth.

When you begin to trust your body again, everything changes, especially how you relate to work, time, and power.

If you do only one thing from this chapter, do this:
Pause when shame shows up in your body.
(Holding your breath? Clenching your jaw? Tightening your shoulders?)
Name it without trying to fix it.
Shame loosens when it's met with awareness instead of performance.

3.

The Perfectionism Trap

I've been trying to write this book for years. *Years.* My laptop is full of title ideas, half-considered outlines, near-complete chapters, and four documents named some version of "Book." I abandoned all of it because of a voice that said, "Someone else has already said this better." The internal critic left me paralyzed. If I couldn't write a perfect book (undeniably entertaining, academically airtight, sure to please everyone), then I shouldn't write anything at all. The irony isn't lost on me that this chapter on perfectionism almost didn't exist because of it.

This isn't the first time perfectionism has shaped my choices. There was the time I didn't even apply to my dream university because I was afraid of what it would say about me if I didn't get in, or the years I stayed committed to a life that looked perfect to others but didn't feel like mine, and so many amazing business offers I kept to myself because they felt good but not "good enough."

Over time, through hard conversations, good therapy, generous teachers, and friends who refused to let me hide, I started to understand that liberatory work isn't perfect work. It's messy. Every time I choose to keep writing, I feel a little less owned by the system that taught me to doubt myself in the first place. I didn't suddenly gain a deep well of confidence, but I slowly began to give myself permission to contribute without needing to be the best.

This book isn't meant to be a masterpiece, a best-seller, or *the* conversation about liberation in business. It's only intended to be *part* of the conversation. I don't want to replace anyone's brilliance. I want to be in community with it.

Perfectionism won't decide whether my voice belongs in this conversation. I am. And it doesn't need to decide whether yours belongs. I'm done letting "not perfect yet" be the reason I don't show up. Oppressive systems need us to believe there's no room for us unless we're flawless. The truth is, there's room simply because we exist. That's what this chapter is about.

Perfectionism is Violence

We're taught that those who rise do so by earning their spot. Dominant culture needs this story to justify why a small group sits atop the political, financial, and social hierarchy, while the majority fights for scraps. If those at the top are better, then anyone can earn their way up by becoming better.

This is how perfectionism takes hold. If I'm flawless, I'll be worthy. If I never make a mistake, I'll be taken seriously. If I never give them reason to doubt me, I'll belong. Of course, perfection isn't possible. Even if it were, its pursuit is a trap. It diverts your energy into managing yourself instead of interrogating the system that created an impossible standard in the first place.

The pressure is hardest on those with the most overlapping marginalized identities. For people closest to power, perfectionism can look like ambition. For those furthest from it, perfection becomes armor. To combat the lies that oppressors tell about those they oppress, Dr. Raquel Martin says, "we had to do twice as much, be perfect, go ten times harder, to slam our way into rooms where we had the right to be in the first place."

Over time, the system's story becomes an internal monologue. We stop asking who benefits from the standard and start asking what's wrong with us. Perfectionism keeps us busy proving our worth instead of questioning why worth is rationed at all. You cannot win the perfection game, but those in power definitely want and need you to keep playing it.

For those who hold privilege, the work is to expand your tolerance for messiness, difference, and learning curves. For those with marginalized identities, the work is to release the lie that your humanity must be earned. You don't owe flawlessness to be seen, respected, or believed. Your existence is not an audition. For everyone, the work is to reject the worldview that created perfectionism and the lie that anyone can be "less than."

**journal
your
journey**

What has perfectionism cost me?

In what ways do I hold others to impossible standards?

How would I show up if I believed I was worthy?

What does good enough look like in this season of life?

Perfectionism vs. Healthy Striving

Perfectionism is a survival tactic. In cultures shaped by white supremacy, being "good enough" has never been enough for people without power. Perfectionism becomes a strategy for avoiding punishment.

Liberation isn't "being less perfectionistic." It's no longer performing worthiness. One way to do that is to begin aiming for healthy striving instead of perfection. Here's how to tell the difference in practice:

Perfectionism:	Healthy striving:
Rooted in fear, shame, and hierarchy	Rooted in curiosity, integrity, and connection
Focused on proving worth	Focused on being more aligned
Treats mistakes as evidence you don't belong	Treats mistakes as information for learning
Demands domination of the self ("fix it, hide it, outperform it")	Honors the self ("what am I learning?" "what do I need?")
Confuses compliance with excellence	Values discernment, context, and care
Thrives in isolation and comparison	Grows through community and feedback
Measures success by output and approval	Measures success by alignment and sustainability
Serves systems that reward extraction	Supports systems rooted in dignity and care

In a liberated business, we don't measure ourselves or others by impossible standards. We measure by alignment, integrity, and the capacity to stay in right relationship with ourselves, our communities, and the world we're building. Healthy striving doesn't ask you to disappear or outperform your humanity. It asks you to show up honestly, imperfectly, and in motion.

Unpacking 'Imposter Syndrome'

*with **Taina Brown**, a feminist coach, my business partner, and one of my greatest teachers.*

Becky Mollenkamp: A pair of psychologists coined *imposter phenomenon* in the 1970s to describe feelings of being a fraud.
Taina Brown: When did it go from *phenomenon* to *syndrome?* Somewhere along the way, it was pathologized. Language matters. *Imposter phenomenon* and *imposter syndrome* feel different.

Becky: How do you help your clients reframe these feelings?
Taina: I grew up feeling like an imposter *all the time*, and I think a lot of women of color feel like an imposter from a very young age because the systems we're operating in, especially here in the US, were set up with white men in mind. Sometimes we feel like we don't belong and we're told that's 'imposter syndrome.' But what it really boils down to is belonging. I didn't feel like I belonged with straight people because I'm not straight. As a fat person, I don't feel like I belong in a room full of thin people. That sense of not belonging is something that people of color carry with us everywhere we go. When my clients come to me because they're 'struggling with imposter syndrome,' we turn it around. Let's create a world you belong in. How do we create *your* world?

Becky: What does it mean to build a world you belong in?
Taina: When it comes to imposter syndrome in communities of people who've been historically marginalized or are part of the global majority, it's about building our own systems and communities. How do we build our capacity for things like mutual aid? How do we reinvent those things so we feel we belong, but so people who come after us feel like they belong too? That becomes a model for anyone who's fucking tired of the state of the world as it is.

Becky: How does one even go about creating a sense of belonging?
Taina: It comes from full acceptance of who you are. All the parts of you, even those you may not like. I can be a judgey bitch. For a long time, I was uncomfortable with that. But I'm not going to 100% change it, so I need to accept it's who I am. Being able to accept that can give me agency over *when* I'm a judgey bitch. When I deny that part of myself, I'm denying my agency to choose when and how I'm a judgey bitch.

Micro-Liberations

Perfectionism melts when we stop performing for the hierarchy.

Redefine "good enough" as "aligned enough."
Before you keep polishing, ask: "Is this aligned enough to share?" If yes, stop. Alignment replaces applause as the finish line.

Call out the hierarchy behind the criticism.
When your inner critic speaks ask, "Whose rules are these?" If it's not a person whose values you trust, the standard doesn't get to run the show.

Set a stopping rule.
Decide in advance: "I'll spend 45 minutes on this and then I'm done." Time limits interrupt perfectionism better than insight does.

Let your body set the pace.
When your shoulders tense, breath shortens, or jaw clenches, pause. That's your cue to slow down, step away, or end for the day.

Ship one imperfect thing.
Choose something small (an email, post, boundary, decision) and send it at 80%. Notice what *doesn't* happen afterward.

Create a "good-enough" circle.
Identify one or two people who value honesty over performance. Share unfinished work, half-formed ideas, or doubts there first.

Perfectionism and its sidekick, imposter syndrome, are tools of a system that needs you to believe you're not worthy of more.

You don't need to earn your right to take up space. You don't have to wait until you're flawless to tell your story, build a business, write a book, or reshape your world. Each time you choose truth over performance, connection over comparison, and desire over fear, you weaken the system that taught you to shrink in the first place.

If you do only one thing from this chapter, do this:
Complete something imperfectly on purpose.
Notice where perfection tries to stop or push you.
Let good enough be enough.

4.

Risk and Reward

Growing up, I thought achievement could buy safety. I worked my way up from a reporter at a community newspaper to an editor at a major publishing house. It was the kind of job that made my parents proud, my LinkedIn profile shine, and my life's trajectory feel legitimate. A year after I started, the company went public, ushering in an annual ritual every corporate worker knows well: layoffs.

Each time my colleagues were let go and I wasn't, I felt affirmed that I was doing it "right." After five years, that sense of security felt solid enough that I quit to do the same work as a freelancer. With my contacts and reputation, I assumed clients would always be there. I believed money would keep coming... so I spent like it would.

The lifestyle creep was real. My then-husband and I custom-built a home with high-end finishes. We leased a red BMW. We took international vacations. We regularly dined out. It felt like we had cracked the code. Then came the Great Recession. Work dried up faster than I knew was possible. It exposed the assumptions I hadn't even realized I was making about continuity, demand, and control. What I had experienced as "safety" turned out to be conditional, fragile, and dependent on forces far beyond my influence. It wasn't safe at all.

At the time, I didn't think of this as a lesson about systems. I thought of it as a personal failure. I had played by the rules and still lost, which only made me more determined to figure out where I'd gone wrong. It took years to see that I was asking the wrong question entirely.

The system had rewarded me, so I assumed it was protecting me. The right question wasn't where I had gone wrong; it was whether the system was ever designed to keep me safe in the first place. It wasn't. Capitalism is very good at disguising reward as protection, dangling just enough stability to keep you compliant, then pulling it back without warning and calling that your fault, too.

The risk was never really mine to manage. It was mine to absorb.

Unequal Risk, Unearned Reward

We talk about taking risks as if everyone is standing on the same ground. But as with time and money, risks and rewards are distributed through systems, not meritocracy. Eduardo Bonilla-Silva, author of *Racism Without Racists*, makes it clear that inequality is structural, not the result of individual choices. Risk isn't neutral; it's always experienced in a body with a history. What feels like courage for some is a gamble with survival for others.

Those with more privilege (racial, class, citizenship, ability, etc.) often mistake their relative safety for universal possibility. Our lived experiences shape our sense of what risk is. If you've always had a soft place to land, risk can feel like adventure instead of danger. Capitalism exploits that difference. If everyone were safe, the system would lose its leverage.

When someone says, "you have to take bigger risks to get bigger rewards," remember that story is usually told by people whose losses won't devastate them. Risk is shaped by history, identity, and power. Liberation requires shifting the burden, not pretending the playing field is level. As anti-apartheid activist Desmond Tutu said, "if you are neutral in situations of injustice, you have chosen the side of the oppressor."

Changing your relationship to risk starts with recognizing where you sit:

- If you hold privilege, your work is to redistribute risk, not hoard safety.
- If you hold marginalized identities, your work is to build relationships that resource you, to seek safety in community, and to reject the idea that surviving in an unjust system is a personal failing.
- For everyone, the work is to build communities where safety is shared.

Risk shouldn't require bravery just to survive. When it does, that's a sign of an unjust system. Community is what makes risk survivable, and what makes transformation possible.

	What have you learned about what makes you safe?
journal your journey	Who do you trust enough to share risk with?
	What would safety look like if it were relational?
	What risks feel worth taking if community holds you?

Safety is a Shared Resource

Capitalism tells us safety is earned through smart choices, but liberation movements have shown, over and over, that safety is collective, not individual. The myth of personal safety depends on the fantasy that harm is avoidable if you just make good decisions. In reality, safety is shaped by power.

The Black Panther Party (BPP) understood this deeply. Its Free Breakfast Program, health clinics, community protection efforts, and liberation schools were redistribution projects, not charity. BPP didn't wait for permission; it built what the community needed to stay safe. This can serve as a guide.

Liberationist and one-time BPP member Assata Shakur captured this ethos when she said, "I don't have to live up to that Superwoman myth. I can cry and be human and lean on people who can take care of me. That can be very liberating." She rejected the lie that self-sufficiency means strength, and names interdependence as a source of power.

You were never meant to shoulder risk alone. None of us were. Let's reframe safety through an abolitionist lens as Mia Birdsong does in *How We Show Up*: "creating practices based on an understanding of safety grounded in mutuality and care that says none of us is disposable, all of us should get what we need to live, and the only way you do that is in connected community."

When we stop trying to be the superheroes capitalism demands, and allow ourselves to be held, protected, and supported by community, we begin to experience a different kind of safety—one rooted in humanity. Risk gets redistributed, and safety goes from a prize to a practice.

A coach running a seven-figure firm sought my help to move beyond the fear that expanding her team was "too risky," even though she was drowning in work and earning a consistent profit.

We worked together to craft a decision process that honored her commitment to people-first leadership. She hired two new people at living wages, and fairly redistributed the workload.

She discovered that expansion didn't have to mean risking her business; it could mean redistributing safety for herself and others.

Redefining Risk

What capitalism says is risky:	What's actually risky:
Taking a day off	Treating exhaustion as a plan
Hiring help too soon	Doing everything alone
Raising rates to reflect your needs	Being underpaid because of shame
Saying no to work that drains you	Avoiding conflict
Collaborating, not competing	Being your own only safety net
Not prioritizing growth	Scaling without enough capacity
Asking for support	Normalizing overwork
Leaving corporate "security"	Confusing income with safety
Telling the truth about your limits	Measuring success by productivity

Real risk is anything that costs your humanity. Real safety is built together.

From Emergency to Prevention

Capitalism thinks about safety like emergency medicine. It assumes crisis is inevitable, and the best we can do is respond faster and endure more when things go wrong. Liberation movements think like primary care. They ask what is needed so fewer crises happen in the first place. They prioritize prevention, access, continuity, and relationship. They notice patterns early, ask better questions, and build conditions for better health over time.

Emergency care is vital, but a system that relies on it as the default is already failing. The same is true for safety. When individuals are expected to absorb risk alone, crisis becomes normal and is used to justify extraction, speed, and disposability. Liberation invests in infrastructure instead. Mutual aid, childcare, community protection, and shared knowledge are strategies to reduce harm before it escalates. Infrastructure makes safety less dramatic and more reliable. Safety was never meant to be an emergency response. It was meant to be a condition we create together.

Micro-Liberations

Each tiny act rewrites the story of who deserves safety and why.

Name the real risk.
When a decision feels "risky," pause and finish this sentence: "I'm actually afraid of ______." Fear loses power when it's named correctly.

Build a safety pod.
Gather two or three people you trust not to hype or shame you. Before a big decision, send a short text: "Can you help me think this through?"

Replace certainty with support.
When you catch yourself asking "Is this safe?" ask instead, "Who would support me if this goes awry?" If there's no one, that's the work.

Budget for rest the way you budget for rent.
Treat rest like a non-negotiable line item, not a luxury you earn with effort. Put it in the calendar and protect it.

Redistribute one small resource.
Once a week, share something tangible: an introduction, a link, $10, or a skill. Safety grows through repetition, not grand gestures.

Practice public boundaries.
Let people see you say no, cancel, reschedule, or change your mind. When boundaries become visible, collective safety expands.

Capitalism says safety is earned individually, but liberationists know it's built collectively. No amount of personal responsibility can shield you from systems designed to profit off uncertainty. Collective care is the only antidote.

When we stop carrying it alone, something shifts. Our shoulders drop, our breath returns, and we remember that safety was never meant to be self-funded. It was always meant to be shared, practiced, and protected together. It's how humans have always survived.

5.

The Problem with Scarcity

I've lived my whole life swinging between two extremes when it comes to money—hyper-vigilance and total avoidance. Some seasons, I have spreadsheets for my spreadsheets. I track business income and expenses like a hawk, checking accounts weekly. It feels like seeing the numbers will protect me from disaster. If I can quantify it, maybe I can control it.

Other seasons, I stop looking at the data altogether. I've gone months without checking my bank account because if I avoid it, I can pretend everything is fine. I tell myself I'm too busy, but the reality is that I'm too afraid. My body is reacting to money as if it's a threat, not a tool. What if there isn't enough? What if I screwed everything up? What if the bottom falls out?

It's fight or flight, capitalism style. Both patterns come from the same place: a childhood shaped by a single mom doing everything she could to keep us afloat. I learned early that money disappeared quickly, that emergencies came out of nowhere, and that stability was always one bill or one crisis away from collapsing. Now as an adult with more privilege, the story hasn't left my body.

But that's the point. The system needs me (and you, and everyone) to believe we're always one misstep away from losing everything. That fear keeps us churning, optimizing, sacrificing, and pretending that the 1% is rich because they're better than us, not because the system is designed to funnel resources upward. Scarcity is capitalism's most effective con, and it doesn't want to be solved. Capitalism needs winners and losers, or the game breaks. It's why you can make six figures and still feel broke.

Scarcity's job is to make sure no one ever feels safe enough to stop producing. And, wow, is it good at its job. It trains our nervous systems to confuse constant motion with stability. If any of this feels familiar, it's not a personal failing; it's what a system built on extraction requires. But always bracing and never settling for enough is a hard, lonely way to live.

Manufactured Lack

Capitalism built a world with real abundance, and then privatized it. There's enough food, but we throw away nearly 40% of it. There's enough wealth, but it's hoarded by 1% of people. There are enough hours, but we spend them enriching corporations' bottom lines.

Scarcity is a tool of oppression, not a natural condition. "Fear and scarcity are a big part of how the culture keeps us bound up in the hamster wheel," wrote Tricia Hersey in *Rest is Resistance*. When we blame ourselves for never having enough, we don't question why so much is withheld in the first place.

Scarcity shows up in our thoughts, bodies, and systems. It can show up as:

- Personal shame: I should've saved more. I should be farther along.
- Moral hierarchy: The rich are worthy. The poor are worthless.
- False urgency: Buy now or miss out.

And even if you do get more, the goalpost moves. As Audre Lorde said in *Sister Outsider*, "the machine will try to grind you into dust anyway, whether or not we speak." However, liberation is not found by simply swapping scarcity for greed. "Greed subsumes love and compassion; living simply makes room for them… We can all resist the temptation of greed," bell hooks said.

Liberation is refusing to accept that the world must be divided into haves and have nots. It's insisting that there's more than enough for everyone when we stop forcing resources to be individually accumulated. It's a return to collectivism. Shared resources have sustained marginalized communities for generations. "I don't believe in self-care, I believe in collective care, collectivizing our care, and thinking more about how we can help each other," said Mariame Kaba in *We Do This 'Til We Free Us*.

When we release the lie that we must secure our own survival at the expense of others, we make space for love, compassion, and connection.

<table>
<tr><td rowspan="4">journal
your
journey</td><td>Where did I learn that more is the same as safe?</td></tr>
<tr><td>Who benefits when I believe there's not enough?</td></tr>
<tr><td>What does scarcity feel like in my body?</td></tr>
<tr><td>What would enough feel like in my body?</td></tr>
</table>

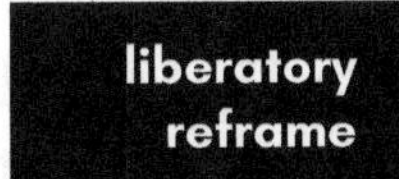

Taking Nature's Lead

Capitalism tells us that the world runs on scarcity (of time, money, opportunity, resources, belonging), but as Indigenous author Robin Wall Kimmerer teaches in *Braiding Sweetgrass* and *The Serviceberry*, Earth has always run on reciprocity. Scarcity is an oppression strategy, not natural law. It's a story told to justify hoarding, hierarchy, and extraction by convincing us that there simply isn't enough to go around.

Nothing in nature hoards what it doesn't need. A squirrel stores enough to survive the winter, not beyond. Nothing in nature grows for the sake of growth. A tree doesn't try to become the whole forest.

True abundance, Kimmerer says, happens via circulation and reciprocity. Different plant species that need different nutrients create more resources by sharing them with each other. A stream doesn't drink its own water, and a tree doesn't eat its fruit; the resources serve others in the system.

This isn't generosity or moral goodness. It's ecological intelligence that ensures survival of the whole. When we internalize scarcity, we behave like we're cut off from the web of life. When we practice reciprocity, we return to it. Capitalism breaks this web on purpose. It isolates us, privatizes survival, and then calls dependence a failure.

When access to food, rest, care, and safety is severed from community, commodified, and sold back to us individually, scarcity feels inevitable instead of engineered. We forget that survival was never meant to be a solo project. Scarcity thrives when relationships are fractured. Reciprocity thrives when we remember we belong to one another.

In *Emergent Strategy*, adrienne maree brown says nature teaches us "what we practice at the small scale, sets the patterns for the whole system." If we want to create a more just world, then our money practices must echo the natural world:

- Growth is cyclical, not constant.
- Surplus circulates and doesn't stagnate.
- Enough is a boundary and a blessing.
- Thriving is measured by the health of the whole, not individual wealth.

Scarcity culture tells you there isn't enough, protect what's yours, you're on your own. Liberatory practice whispers the truth: Your well-being is tied to mine because "all flourishing is mutual."

The Binary is a Lie

Capitalism loves binaries (rich/poor, have/have not, worthy/worthless) because they keep us comparing, competing, and terrified of slipping into the "bad" category. Reality and liberation live in the messy middle. Nuance slows us down, which makes it terrible for extraction and wonderful for humanity.

Instead of...	Try holding...
I'm succeeding *or* I'm behind	I can grow *and* rest at the same time
I have enough *or* I'm failing	I can be grateful *and* want change
I love my work *or* I'm burned out	I can care deeply *and* need distance
I'm ambitious *or* I'm lazy	I can move slowly *and* be powerful
I'm thriving *or* I'm struggling	I can be **both**, even in the same hour
I have it all together *or* I'm a mess	I'm a whole human with many truths

The goal isn't choosing sides, it's choosing wholeness.

liberation in action

For years, I taught a Money Mindset course. The premise was simple: focus on abundance to attract abundance (i.e., *manifestation*). Hundreds of people enrolled and the testimonials were glowing. It helped people, but as I deepened my liberation practice, it increasingly felt out of alignment. I could no longer ignore Black feminist and anti-capitalist educators like Rachel Cargle who said: "Maybe you manifested it, maybe it's white privilege."

My program framed wealth as a mindset issue vs. a structural one. I told people they could believe their way into financial ease, ignoring the violent inequities of white-supremacist capitalist patriarchy. The program was incomplete, so I ended it. Ending a profitable offer felt risky *and* it felt like integrity. Liberation is being willing to let go of something, no matter how successful, when you realize it's harmful. Being willing to change your mind. Being willing to grow publicly.

<h1 style="text-align:center">Micro-Liberations</h1>

Try these practices to loosen scarcity's grip and remember how *enough* feels.

Redefine wealth.
Write down what you need to feel financially, emotionally, energetically stable. Scarcity thrives when the goalpost is "more."

Audit your more.
When you think, I need more _______, ask: "What do I actually need to feel safe or satisfied?" Often it's not more, it's different.

Practice collective receiving.
The next time help is offered, don't minimize. Say "thanks" and allow it. Interdependence only works if receiving counts as participation.

Interrupt comparison in real time.
When you find yourself comparing (income, impact, visibility), ask whether it's your desire or capitalism's script. Reclaim the narrative.

Track what's already enough.
At the end of the day, write down three things that were sufficient. Not amazing or impressive, but just enough.

Choose sufficiency for one day.
For 24 hours, don't try to get ahead. Just maintain, and notice the discomfort that rises. That tension is the system leaving your body.

The antidote to scarcity isn't wealth, it's belonging. That's because abundance isn't a bank balance or even a perfectly calm nervous system. It's the quiet knowing that you don't have to scramble for your humanity.

Rather than trying to outrun scarcity, let's unlearn it altogether. Liberation is knowing that abundance is something we can create together. It's building lives and businesses that practice enoughness in public. And it's remembering that you already have and *are* enough to matter.

Before I Had the Language

Capitalism doesn't just shape our businesses. It shapes our sense of worth, nervous systems, and ideas about what kind of life is possible. Long before we choose our pricing, marketing strategies, or growth goals, we're taught who "deserves" ease, safety, and belonging, and who must earn them.

We aren't explicitly taught to call this capitalism. We're taught to blame ourselves instead, to believe that if we were just smarter, more productive, more confident, calmer, etc., *then* we'd finally feel secure. This book starts with a simple premise: You're not the problem, the system is. I didn't always have language for any of this. For most of my life, I thought the problem was *me* ... and that belief shaped everything.

Growing up, I heard a lot of negative comments about my appearance. By 4th grade, I heard that I needed to "watch what I eat." I knew early on that I wasn't "the pretty one." I also wasn't the "athletic one." I never played sports or exercised. A boy made fun of how I ran in the 5th grade, and that comment kept me from running at all until my 30s. And I knew I wasn't the "rich one." Raised by a single, financially struggling mom, I was lower middle class (at best) in an area where many of my friends got cars for their 16th birthdays. And it wasn't easy for me to be the "popular one." I moved seven times by age 12 and, given that I'm deeply introverted, I struggled to make and maintain friendships. I wasn't the "troubled one" either. That role belonged to my younger brother, who lived with ADD, ODD, bipolar disorder, and eventually addiction. That put a lot of attention on him, and created a heavy expectation that I not add any more trouble onto my mom's very full plate.

I found my role as the "smart one."

✓ I was put in the "gifted" program in elementary school.

✓ I didn't earn less than a B in school.

✓ I served as editor-in-chief of my high school and college newspapers.

✔ I was on honor roll, and graduated high school with honors.

✔ I graduated high school already having 21 college credits.

✔ Thanks to those credits, I finished college in 3 years.

At every step along the way, I received praise (from my family and teachers) for being smart. This led to a lifetime of chasing gold stars. It was the only way I knew to fill my cup of worthiness. It also led to a habit of avoiding anything that might disprove my intelligence. I only attempted what I was pretty sure I could achieve, and quit anything I couldn't immediately master.

At age 25, I landed a job as an editor at *Better Homes and Gardens* magazine. With a readership of 40+ million at the time (the largest of any publication), my name could be found in nearly every aisle of every grocery store in America. It felt great, for a bit. Gradually, though, I came to the stinging realization that nothing had really changed in how I felt about myself. My worthiness cup seemed to have a hole in the bottom. No matter how much I filled it with achievements, it didn't stay full.

When I turned 30, I felt an overwhelming sense of "is this all there is?" That existential dread pushed me to quit my cushy-but-unfulfilling job to be my own boss as a freelance writer. My existing network made it easy to find work, and I made six figures in my first year of self employment. I hoped becoming the "rich one" would fill my cup. I bought designer labels and leased a shiny BMW. I built a 3,500-square-foot custom home with the best finishes. I took regular vacations and built up a sizable nest egg. My life looked amazing on paper, and to everyone around me. And still my cup was empty.

By the time I turned 33, the "is this all there is?" dread had morphed into "what if it never gets better?" panic. I accelerated my efforts to fill that damn cup by trying to be the "athletic one" and the "popular one" and the "pretty one" all at once. I decided that running hundreds of miles a month would kill all the birds with one stone. I'd be a real athlete, I'd get thin (which I believed was a synonym for pretty), and I'd be the source of much male attention (which I thought was a synonym for popular). It worked. I became obsessed with running and exercise and went from a size 18 to a size 2 in less than 2 years. Men definitely noticed, and I soaked up their praise. In a desperate attempt to feel desirable, I crossed boundaries I'd once believed I never would, cheating on my then husband. And my cup of worthiness became the driest it had ever been.

It's incredibly lonely to feel so unhappy and so unworthy, and not have any idea why or how to fix it, especially when everyone else thinks your life looks so perfect. By the time I turned 35, I was reaching a breaking point. I'd gone from dread to panic to despair. I felt trapped.

Then in the early morning hours of July 4, 2010—after I had stumbled home from a drunken night with a man I was now having a weeks-long affair with—I got the phone call that would forever change my life. "I have some upsetting news," my dad said in the understatement of a lifetime. "Your brother died." I knew without being told it was a heroin overdose. He was 30. That call shattered the story I'd been living inside. It exposed how thin my sense of safety really was, and how little the life I'd built could hold real grief.

I was taught to confuse worth with productivity, safety with money, and belonging with performance. Those rules shaped me long before I ever ran a business, and long before I had language for what was happening.

Section 2

Unlearning the Money-Work-Worth
Connection

If Section 1 was about the air we've been breathing, Section 2 is about the currents that keep pulling us under.

Capitalism doesn't just shape how we see ourselves, it also shapes how we understand money, time, attention, and connection. These are the core currencies of the system, and we're taught to treat all of them as scarce, slippery, and transactional. Work harder. Earn more. Move faster. Get visible. Stay visible. Never stop producing. Never stop proving. Wash, rinse, repeat.

This section exposes the machinery behind those messages. We'll unpack why six figures didn't save you, why monetization culture turned creativity into content, why productivity became a moral identity, and how both time and attention were weaponized against your nervous system. We'll look at how relationships got reduced to leverage, how community became a marketing strategy, and how even the concept of networking got colonized.

These chapters aren't about rejecting ambition. They're about reclaiming the truth. You were never meant to be a machine. You were meant to be in relationship. Once you see the lie, you can stop living inside it.

6.

The Six-Figure Lie

The first time I crossed six figures in my business, I expected the heavens to part. I expected certainty, relief, safety. Maybe even a hint of "arrival." In fact, nothing really changed, other than getting a lot easier to be a perfect capitalist consumer. I could buy nicer things without checking my bank balance, and take off on twice-yearly beach vacations.

But my nervous system? Same wreck. My relationship to work? Same anxiety. My belief that one wrong move could send it all crashing down? Somehow even louder. Now there was more to protect and more to lose. The stakes got higher, but the ground beneath me stayed just as unstable.

The six-figure milestone didn't deliver security. It only delivered clearer evidence that capitalism never intended for me to feel secure in the first place. The truth? You don't feel safe when you hit six figures. You just get a nicer flavor of fear, a more socially acceptable version of scarcity. I continued to check my bank account with dread, still tied my worth to my productivity, and kept believing the lie that the next revenue tier would be the one to finally unlock the good life.

Six figures didn't make me free. It just made me better at performing success in a system designed to keep me hungry and exhausted. Capitalism perpetuates the six-figure narrative because it brands freedom as a personal achievement, not a collective right. It whispers, "You'll earn your safety if you just work harder, hustle smarter, package better, sell more." But safety isn't something you earn, and freedom isn't a revenue milestone.

What actually changed my life wasn't money, it was unlearning the belief that I could buy my way out of fear. I began to see that no matter how much we earn, we're never safe inside a system built on precarity. Six figures didn't change me. Liberation did. This chapter is unpacks why money was never the thing we were promised it would be, and what actually builds safety instead.

49

Can Enough Ever Be Enough?

Capitalism conditions us to believe that safety is one revenue tier above where we currently stand, and that more is the only path to happiness and worthiness.

The bar for "enough" always moves, a phenomenon sociologists call "the hedonic treadmill." People continually adjust expectations upward, making sufficiency impossible by definition. You earn six figures and now you want to hit seven. You reach your goal follower count, and suddenly it doesn't feel big enough. As philosopher Epicurus said, "nothing is sufficient for the person who finds sufficiency too little."

The treadmill effect is the natural result of a system that conditions people to judge their worth on what they earn and spend. And it's an intentional feature of an economic system that requires perpetual dissatisfaction to function. If people ever felt "done," growth would stall, so desire is constantly re-stimulated.

Anthropologists and liberationists argue that humans are more resilient and resourceful than capitalist culture needs us to believe. Their claims are backed by research. Once a person's basic needs are met (food, housing, healthcare), any increase in income has a rapidly diminishing impact on well-being.

Liberation reframes the goal from accumulation to sufficiency. Resisting the pressure to constantly stretch, scale, expand, acquire, and optimize is a refusal to let capitalism define your worth. Endeavoring for enough isn't settling or complacency. It's a radical act that allows for the redistribution of resources for the collective good. When you have enough to live, care for your people, and support your body and spirit, the question can shift from "How do I get more?" to "What can this surplus make possible for others?"

The moment you decide enough is possible, you stop being easy to control. Anything beyond "enough" shifts from personal success to collective possibility. Enough isn't a smaller dream, it's a freer one.

journal your journey	In what ways have you tied your identity to income?
	How does it feel to think about earning more?
	What does "enough" look like in real numbers?
	How would you define "success" without money?

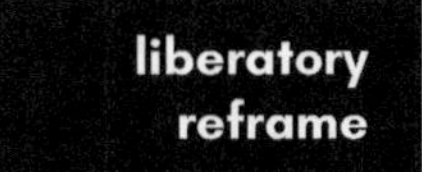

Stop the Endless Chase for More

Capitalism treats six (or seven or eight) figures like a finish line, but it's more like a leash. It keeps you tethered to labor, comparison, and consuming. It creates a false binary that either you're ambitious *or* you're settling. Liberation offers a third path—enoughness rooted in dignity, not digits.

In *The Serviceberry*, Robin Wall Kimmerer writes that "recognizing 'enoughness' is a radical act in an economy that is always urging us to consume more." In Indigenous gift economies, wealth isn't measured by accumulation but by circulation—how much moves through you, not how much stops with you. "Wealth among traditional people is measured by having enough to give away," Kimmerer writes in *Braiding Sweetgrass*.

In business terms, circulation looks like paying people living (or thriving) wages, sharing credit, funding mutual aid, choosing sustainability over constant expansion. When businesses circulate money, credit, care, and decision-making power, they strengthen the whole ecosystem.

Capitalism calls you free when you can buy more stuff. Success is "he who has the most, wins." Capitalism teaches that money buys safety and freedom. Gift economies call you wealthy when you can help others breathe. Success is "when we all have our needs met, we all win."

Liberation is unlearning the lie that survival requires hoarding of resources, and remembering that abundance is not what we have, but how we live together and take responsibility for one another. Ask yourself: What sustains me? What sustains others? What would change if stability (not scale) was the goal?

Enough isn't small, and it isn't settling. It interrupts the cycle of striving, spending, and self-doubt that fuels toxic capitalism. When you believe there's always another tier to reach, you'll tolerate exhaustion, inequality, and instability, and reframe it as ambition. Liberation is remembering that abundance isn't what you have but how you live and for whom you take responsibility. That's not a smaller life. It's a freer one.

Once you stop chasing endless growth and start practicing reciprocity, you stop living like a capitalist and start living like kin. You can stop chasing someone else's six-figure finish line, and start building a life that feels like yours.

Growth that costs your humanity is too expensive.

Unpacking Pricing

*with **Jacquette M. Timmons**, a financial behaviorist who helps her clients build better money behaviors.*

Becky Mollenkamp: 'Charge what you're worth' sounds empowering. What's the problem with that language?

Jacquette M. Timmons: I have an ancestral history where there was a dollar amount attached to someone's humanity. That phrase doesn't recognize the harm it can do to folks who have a history like mine. The other reason I don't like it is because it misses the point. Your price is a reflection of a whole bunch of things, including your education, expertise, gifts, talents, and perspective. None of it has to do with your worth as a human being.

Becky: Pricing a service can feel pretty arbitrary, more art than science.

Jacquette: Far too often, we benchmark our pricing against what others are doing, without asking, 'what do I need money to do for me?' That's how you get to a less abstract number than staring at a blank piece of paper and writing down a random number. We also often forget about invisible expenses. If you're a coach, you might spend an hour on a call with a client, but what about all the time you reflect on your conversation, consider what to talk about next, or connect them to people?

Becky: Do one-size-fits-all pricing formulas work?

Jacquette: Business, money, and pricing are personal. And they're political and emotional. If you don't factor in the cultural, the systemic factors that influence the way we experience money, then you can't tell me that it's just a mathematical problem to be solved. The Dave Ramseys of the world make no room for circumstances that are beyond people's direct control. 'You dug this hole and you have to deal with it.' That does a lot of damage—emotionally, psychically, and from a confidence standpoint.

Becky: What does *wealth* mean to you?

Jacquette: It's not a number. Wealth is options. It's having the finances that allow you to do what you want to do, how and when you want to do it.

Grieving the Dream

Before you can choose enough, you may need to grieve the version of success you were promised. You worked hard for that number. You sacrificed sleep, relationships, and weekends for it. You told yourself it would be worth it. It's okay (even likely) that letting the dream go stings.

Give yourself permission to mourn the milestone before you release it. That might look like writing a breakup letter to the six-figure goal (what you wanted it to mean, what you gave up chasing it, and what you're choosing instead). It might look like telling someone you trust that you're done performing ambition you don't actually feel. It might look like sitting with the discomfort instead of immediately replacing one goal with another.

You don't have to rush to the liberation part. The grieving is part of it, and a sign you were human enough to hope.

Enough Lives in Your Body

Enough isn't just a number. It's a nervous system state. Which column do you recognize yourself in most right now? That's the starting point, not the ceiling.

Your nervous system on scarcity:	Your nervous system on enough:
Chest tight, breath shallow	Breath drops into your belly
Dread when looking at financials	Curiosity when looking at financials
Rest feels dangerous	Rest feels necessary
Your worth ebbs with your income	Your worth stays steady regardless

Try This Right Now (It Takes 60 Seconds)
Sit down and take a break. Feel the weight of your body. Take one long, slow breath in through your nose. Hold it for just a moment. Then let it go through your mouth. Now ask your body: What would it feel like to have enough in this moment? Notice what shifts in your body and mind. That feeling is available to you today, without hitting any goals. Capitalism spent years convincing you it wasn't. This is what taking it back feels like.

The Enoughness Challenge

Enough is not decided once. It's practiced over time, in relationship with your life as it actually is. This one-month challenge gives you one simple act each week to define and live into *your* vision of enough.

Week 1: Name Your Enough

Write down what "enough" looks like for you in three areas: money (a specific number), time (hours you actually want to work), and energy (what depletes vs. sustains you). Keep it somewhere visible all week. Every time you feel the pull to do or earn more, look at it and ask: am I already there?

Week 2: Find the Lie

Pick one belief you hold about money or success, something like "I need six figures to feel safe" or "resting means falling behind." Spend the week reflecting: Where did this come from? Who benefits when I believe this? Write one sentence that replaces the belief with something truer to you.

Week 3: Choose Enough Once a Day

Each day, make one small decision based on sufficiency instead of scarcity. Say no to something that doesn't align. Stop a task when it's good enough. Take the break. Let the goal be to collect seven small moments of choosing yourself over the system.

Week 4: Circulate the Surplus

Find one way to move something you have (money, a connection, credit, time, a skill) toward someone else. Then sit with this question: What becomes possible for others when I redistribute what I have more than enough of?

Enoughness isn't a finish line. It's a practice you return to, especially when the world tells you to want more. Repeat this challenge as often as needed to remind yourself that you get to decide what enough looks like for you, and that deciding once doesn't have to be the end.

Micro-Liberations

Micro moves to help you practice enough in a world that demands more.

Name your "enough."
Define what sustains your life and work (income, energy, support, hours). Before chasing a new goal, check it against the list.

Let surplus circulate.
When you have more than you need, decide where 10-20% can go (mutual aid, wages, community projects). Circulation requires intention.

Treat growth as seasonal.
At the start of each quarter, name the season you're in: planting, tending, harvesting, or resting. Let that determine your pace.

Track well-being alongside revenue.
Once a week, rate your energy, capacity, and connection (1 to 5). If revenue is rising while well-being is dropping, that's a warning.

Build a "needs-first" budget.
List what sustains your body, people, and craft before allocating money to growth. Let anything beyond that be a choice, not a reflex.

Share decision-making.
Identify one decision you usually make alone and invite someone else into it. Shared power reduces pressure.

The lie that freedom is just one income bracket away is designed to keep us exhausted from chasing the next milestone. Enoughness interrupts the spell by forcing a forbidden question: Who benefits from me never feeling done?

When you define what sustains you, you begin to separate your worth from your wealth. You stop contorting yourself to meet someone else's definition of success, and start building a life that reflects your values. Enoughness isn't shrinking your ambition, it's reclaiming your agency.

If you do only one thing from this chapter, do this:
Redefine success in a way that doesn't require you to abandon yourself.
Then, read this sentence slowly:
My worth does not increase when my income does.

7.

Beyond Monetization

When I have a creative idea, my brain doesn't ask, "Do I want this?" It asks, "Can I sell this?" It happens so fast I often don't even notice. I'm an idea machine, and capitalism has trained me to run my ideas through a mental profit-and-loss spreadsheet before checking in with my desire. This reflex hollows out joy. It's like standing in front of an open door and immediately asking how to charge admission.

As an example, I started a podcast because I was excited to talk with other feminists. It felt fun. After one season, I killed it. Not because I didn't love it, but because there weren't enough downloads to make it "worth it."

The conditioning isn't relegated only to traditional business ideas. As an example, I regularly receive compliments on a painting I made for my office. A normal response would be to say "thanks." My brain jumps to thinking about how to make and sell them. Never mind that I don't want to be a professional artist. The reflex to turn everything into a revenue stream is automatic. There's always a low hum of "maybe I could monetize" running at all times.

Recently, something different happened. I had an idea to gather some of the most brilliant and interesting people I know for a salon-style gathering. I had the familiar itch to monetize, but I stopped myself. I probably could have charged for it, but that would have changed it. It was a beautiful gift for me and the attendees. People left feeling seen and connected, not sold to. And I was reminded that I can create things that never touch my Stripe account. Not everything needs an invoice.

I'm not alone in this. I hear it in how entrepreneurs talk about hobbies, rest, and even relationships. Capitalism tells us that if it doesn't make money, it doesn't matter. This chapter is about unlearning that reflex and remembering that some of the most important things we build lose their power when we turn them into products. Some things are meant to be sacred, not scalable.

The Evolution of Commerce

For most of human history, commerce looked very different than it does today. As anthropologist James Suzman writes in *Work: A Deep History*, early humans lived in societies where exchange was grounded in reciprocity, relationship, and survival—not profit. Hunter-gatherer communities worked only a few hours a day and spent the rest in rest, ritual, and connection.

Agricultural societies brought the first hierarchies. Once humans could store grain, they could hoard it. Ownership (of land and people) replaced relational exchange with extractive control. Work remained seasonal and disconnected from identity until the Industrial Revolution transformed time into a commodity, workers into replaceable units, and labor into the central measure of value. Then came neoliberalism and the idea that every aspect of life can be packaged and sold. By the late 20th century, consumer culture exploded.

This history matters because it shapes what we think about work. Capitalism required people to internalize work as identity in order to function. When labor becomes who you are, opting out feels like failure instead of freedom.

When you find yourself asking if you can monetize everything, it's not a personal flaw or even an entrepreneurial instinct. It's centuries of conditioning. But you're allowed to have parts of your life that capitalism doesn't touch. All ideas don't need to become revenue. All curiosities don't need an audience.

Before commerce was transactional, it was relational. Choosing a purpose that honors humanity over monetization isn't naïve or impractical. It's a return and a refusal. As educator Saidiya Hartman reminds us, liberation requires "a radical divestment in the project of whiteness and a redistribution of wealth and resources ... the abolition of capitalism. What is required is a remaking of the social order, and nothing short of that is going to make a difference." One way to begin is refusing to let capitalism swallow every corner of your life.

<table>
<tr><td rowspan="4">journal
your
journey</td><td>What ideas did I abandon for not making money?</td></tr>
<tr><td>What would I keep doing if it never made a dollar?</td></tr>
<tr><td>What could I reclaim if I didn't need to monetize time?</td></tr>
<tr><td>If my surplus was a shared resource, where might it go?</td></tr>
</table>

A Natural Approach

Capitalism defines success as bigger, faster, more. We can choose a different definition. In *Emergent Strategy*, adrienne maree brown shows us that "adaptation and evolution depend more upon critical, deep, and authentic connections, a thread that can be tugged for support and resilience."

What if we used nature as a guide for how we do commerce? brown's framework offers a way forward:

1. Fractal: Each "small" financial decision (pricing offers, paying contractors) creates the economic world we build.

2. Adaptive: Money strategies can shift with our seasons; revenue plans don't have to be rigid to be legitimate.

3. Interdependence + decentralization: Shared power means shared resources, transparent pay, and redistributing surplus.

4. Non-linear + iterative: Your business model can evolve through tiny experiments vs. big monetized leaps.

5. Resilience + transformative justice: Financial decisions can repair harm (living wages, mutual aid), not just maximize margin.

6. Creating more possibilities: Money can fund art, rest, and resistance.

When money follows relationship instead of domination, growth stops being the goal and well-being becomes the measure.

A client dreamed of supporting local groups by serving on boards and hosting fundraisers, but felt her business had to be the priority. A shift happened when she realized community care wasn't stealing time from her business, but that it was also a legitimate expression of her leadership.

When she stopped treating it as extracurricular and made it part of her workweek, everything softened. Liberation wasn't adding another commitment. It was letting enoughness guide her calendar.

Unpacking Capitalist Conditioning

*with **Toi Smith**, a strategist/educator whose work explores the intersections of capitalism and liberation.*

Becky Mollenkamp: You say there must be a heartbeat beyond money when running a business. Why?

Toi Smith: We need meaning to stay connected to our work. It's important that your business is profitable so you can take care of your responsibilities. But what else do you want your work to do for you and the world?

Becky: Is capitalism a business issue or a societal problem?

Toi: Capitalism is more than an economic system, it's a way of existing. Capitalism had to strip people of so much identity. We were once stewards of the land; it was stolen and privatized, and people turned into workers. Think about the trauma and grief that causes. It informs how we do relationships, love, parenting, life, everything.

Becky: What was your journey of unlearning capitalism?

Toi: I was laid off two times, once while caring for my sick child. I didn't have the language yet, but it felt extractive and exploitative. I went to work for myself, read about power dynamics, and my work started transforming.

Becky: Are entrepreneurs necessarily capitalists?

Toi: We're so heavily indoctrinated under the corporatization of capitalism that entrepreneurs often take the top-down hierarchy into their businesses. They believe they have power over contractors or employees because it's *their* business. But you're not a capitalist for making money or desiring to live well.

Becky: What advice do you give to entrepreneurs who want to be liberatory?

Toi: Capitalism requires perpetual growth. But do you really need to make more than last year? Maybe you do need to grow, but it has to be rooted in real need. If liberation is a value, then your money practices need to be liberatory. If you make money beyond what you need to live well, then the surplus has to go out. You can't accumulate it.

Reimagining Commerce

Long before capitalism, people survived through collective care. These aren't radical ideas, they are ancient ideas we've been taught to forget.

Bartering

Older than money, bartering is alive and well. Swap childcare for editing help. Exchange bookkeeping for art. Bartering defies the story that it's only valuable if money changes hands.

Mutual Aid

Give what you can, receive what you need. This can look like direct giving, community funds, neighbors covering groceries, friends paying a bill without needing a receipt. Mutual aid recognizes that scarcity is manufactured, and that abundance grows through circulation.

Sliding Scale and Equitable Pricing

Financial resources are not equitable, and that doesn't change someone's worth. Equity-based pricing lets people self-identify their economic reality and participate without shame. This expands access without exploiting you or your customers.

Collective Financial Goals

Instead of "hit 6 figures," imagine goals like: cover everyone's living wage, build a shared sick leave fund, pay collaborators transparently and generously, fund a community resource together. Collective goals move us out of "how do *I* win?" and into "how do *we* thrive?"

Redistribution

Saying you value justice means nothing without redistribution. This can look like setting a monthly giving amount, circulating windfalls, or earmarking a portion of surplus revenue for Black-, Brown-, queer-, disabled-, and community-led work. Redistribution is how we interrupt the hoarding reflex that capitalism rewards.

Mine or Monetization?

Before putting a price tag on a creation, see if it checks the boxes. You get to decide how many boxes are acceptable. This is a discernment tool, not a test.

- ☐ I'm not turning this into an offer to soothe a worthiness wound.
- ☐ The desire to monetize this is mine (not a belief that I'm falling behind).
- ☐ I'd still want to do this even if no one buys it.
- ☐ Charging for this won't distort its joy, purpose, or intimacy.
- ☐ This aligns with the business I'm trying to build.
- ☐ It also aligns with the season of life I'm in right now.
- ☐ I can deliver this without overworking myself or my team.
- ☐ This does not require me to abandon my boundaries for profitability.
- ☐ If this offering were a relationship, it would feel reciprocal, not extractive.

<table>
<tr><td>journal
your
journey</td><td>Is this offering a contribution or a performance?

What am I afraid will happen if I don't monetize this?

Where do I feel expansion (or contraction) about this?

How could I make this smaller, slower, or softer?</td></tr>
</table>

Your Non-Monetized Menu

Everything you're good at or enjoy doesn't have to become a product. Joy shouldn't need to earn its keep! Choose 3 to 5 things that you refuse to monetize, and name why you choose to protect them:

I don't monetize _________________ because it doesn't need an audience.

I don't monetize _________________ because it keeps my creativity sustainable.

I don't monetize _________________ because it's a resource to freely circulate.

I don't monetize _________________ because it feels like play, not pressure.

I don't monetize _________________ because it's an experiment, not an asset.

I don't monetize _________________ because _________________________.

Micro-Liberations

Let these small shifts remind you that your ideas don't exist to earn.

Let one thing be a hobby.
Pick one activity and make a clear rule: no monetizing. If the urge to turn it into a business shows up, don't act on it.

Delay monetization.
When a new idea pops up, wait 30 days before deciding if it becomes an offer. Most impulses don't survive the pause.

Decline one "easy" upsell.
When you're tempted to add "just one more offer," pause and ask: "Does this add stability or just noise?" If it's noise, don't launch it.

Tell yourself the truth about your numbers.
Write down the amount you need to live well and pay people well. Use that number as your anchor instead of six- or seven-figure fantasies.

Give without telling anyone.
Support a person, cause, or project this month and don't share it publicly. No screenshots or stories. Let generosity stay relational.

Hide one metric.
Remove one performance metric (followers, downloads, revenue) from daily view. Check it weekly or monthly instead.

Monetization culture wants your brilliance and labor on demand. But you were not born to feed the machine. You can decide what parts of your life remain sacred, what is work, and what is wonder.

When you stop evaluating every idea for its profit potential, you make space for something far more powerful—meaning, connection, pleasure, creativity. The most radical thing you can do is build a business with a heartbeat beyond money. Let the work be enough.

If you do only one thing from this chapter, do this:
Create or pursue one idea without asking whether it could make money.
Remember that you're allowed to have ideas that stay ideas.

8.

Network vs. Net Worth

When I became an entrepreneur, I bought into the cliché that "your network is your net worth." I wanted to be invited into the best rooms and the most impressive collaborations. I chased clout.

Eventually, I got asked into some of the rooms I craved—and they were awful. They reenacted the same capitalist bullshit I'd experienced at Chamber of Commerce breakfasts I'd attended early in my career. But now it was wrapped in a pretty empowerment bow and sold as sisterhood. They talked about community, but what they really worshipped was proximity to power.

I went looking for something different, and joined a community run by a popular Black coach. While the space was less white (a welcome change), the ideas were largely the same (the main difference was replacing men with women at the top of the capitalist hierarchy). That's when I really understood that *diverse* isn't the same as *liberatory*. Representation without redistribution is just reshuffling who dominates. Liberation can't exist inside systems that still require winners and losers.

It became clear that I wasn't going to find the rooms I wanted to be in, so I had to build them. To do that I had to:

- Understand how privilege shapes who feels belonging in a space.
- Learn to be in community across difference without causing harm.
- Redistribute access vs. hoarding the tiny pockets of power I had.
- Create rooms where connection wasn't contingent on clout.

Becoming a builder and a connector wasn't a branding move; it was a values decision. It was the only way to stop replicating the same systems I want to dismantle. It meant choosing slower growth over easier validation.

Had I stayed in those "impressive" rooms, I might have made more money. But it wouldn't have made me or anyone more free. This chapter is about what happens when we build networks rooted in care, reciprocity, and shared power.

Access is Not Accidental

People tend to connect with others who look like them and have similar levels of access and safety. In the business world, this creates homogenous networks that circulate opportunities internally while shutting others out. Referral culture often functions like an "old boys' club" where access is granted through proximity, familiarity, and comfort. Inequality reproduces itself quietly, without anyone saying the racist, sexist, ableist part out loud.

When hiring, funding, mentorship, and visibility flow through these channels, people who already hold privilege get more chances with less effort. Those with marginalized identities are left to navigate closed doors, biased decision-making, and higher scrutiny (and then told to do more networking).

The internet can expand access, but research shows that online networking is also negatively affected by implicit bias. People with marginalized identities face lower response rates, fewer introductions, less access to and interaction with decision makers, and more gatekeeping of knowledge.

This is why phrases like "your network is your net worth" and "it's not what you know, it's who you know" are problematic. They treat proximity to power as meritocratic, instead of examining how power is protected, concentrated, and passed along through social, economic, and institutional systems.

The good news is that networks are built, not inherited or fixed, which means we can choose whether they continue to hoard power or begin to circulate it. Those with greater access must "fight for other people who might not have the right to fight, or the voice, or the money, or the stature, or the positioning," writes Luvvie Ajayi Jones in *Professional Troublemaker*. And as she reminds us, no one is without a platform—our kin, colleagues, and communities are places where access can either be protected for personal advantage or shared in service of collective liberation.

**journal
your
journey**

How have I benefited from others opening doors for me?

Who feels safe with me, and who might not?

If access is a form of power, how am I sharing it?

What would a decolonized network look like for me?

Networking as Collective Care

Capitalism frames networking as a strategy—work the room, leverage relationships, climb faster. What if there was no ladder to climb, and we instead viewed power as a collective resource? "There is enough attention, care, resource, and connection for all of us to access belonging, to be in our dignity, and to be safe in community," adrienne maree brown wrote in *Emergent Strategy*. That abundance becomes visible only when we stop organizing our relationships around scarcity and competition.

Reframing networking as collective care creates a new set of questions. "Who can help me get ahead?" becomes "how are people held here?" and "what can this relationship do for me?" becomes "what responsibility do I carry because I'm in it?" Connection stops being a means to an end and becomes a shared practice of safety, dignity, and accountability.

Care is not the opposite of power; it's how power is shaped, exercised, and distributed. Liberation recognizes that power already moves through relationships via introductions, invitations, recommendations, silence, and absence. Every network quietly decides whose time is respected, whose labor is invisible, and whose presence is conditional. The collective care model shifts networking from proximity to influence toward circulation of information, opportunity, credit, protection, and support. The goal is to create durability, trust, and resilience so people can stay, not just succeed.

This isn't about being likable, impressive, or well-connected. It's about whether the spaces you move through make it easier for people to belong without shrinking themselves. Your network is not measured by who knows your name. It's measured by who's more resourced and free because of you.

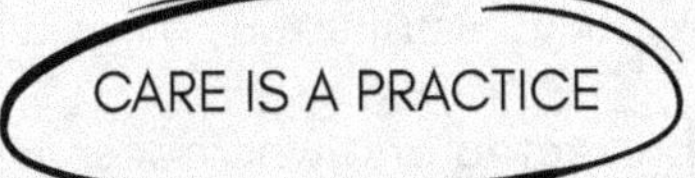

Every network is already practicing something. Notice what's being normalized, who it serves (and doesn't), and what's being asked of people to belong. When care is the frame, neutrality becomes a choice and silence becomes an action.

The Privilege Loop

Familiarity gets mistaken for fit.  **Opportunities circulate inward.**
People invite, hire, recommend, and collaborate with those similar to them. It's framed as "culture," "chemistry," or "trust" instead of racism, sexism, ableism, etc.

Referrals, contracts, introductions, and informal knowledge move through these networks. Access compounds quietly. The same names come up again and again.

Exclusion becomes deniable.
Those outside the network are told to "put themselves out there" or "network more," while the structure that limits access remains the same.

Success is attributed to merit.
Outcomes are credited to talent, effort, or professionalism rather than access. Power is hidden behind the language of fairness.

Each cycle concentrates more power, credibility, and opportunity among the same people, and increases the distance others must travel to be considered. **Interrupting the privilege loop** requires intention:

1. Name familiarity when it's standing in for qualification.
"I trust them" and "they're a good fit" aren't criteria. When familiarity goes unnamed, it shuts people out without anyone having to admit it.

2. Share information before decisions are made.
So much power moves through back channels before anything is posted or announced. If you know something useful, pass it along early.

3. Share credit, not just praise.
Praise feels great, but changes little. Credit opens doors. Say people's names in rooms they're not in. Attribute ideas accurately.

4. Notice who gets protected and who doesn't.
Pay attention to who gets amplified when things go well, and who gets shielded when they don't. Protection is power that flows in one direction.

5. Don't leave belonging up to chance.
Inclusion doesn't accidentally happen. It's the result of clear invitations, shared norms, transparent processes, and accountability.

Micro-Liberations

Small shifts to move your relationships from extraction to reciprocity.

Replace *networking* with *nourishing*.
Before a conversation, ask yourself: "What would make this feel human, not strategic?" Do that.

Notice who's missing.
When you're in a room (or online space), scan for patterns. Interrupt homogeneity by extending invitations beyond your comfort zone.

Keep a "Who needs a boost?" list.
Create a list of people with less access than you. Each month, amplify one by sharing their work, recommending them, or making an introduction.

Practice consent-based connection.
Before introducing two people, ask each person privately if they want the connection. Respect their no without question.

Make introductions warm.
When you connect people, say why you're introducing them and what you appreciate about each. Context builds trust faster than credentials.

Host something that isn't monetized.
Offer a salon, a circle, or a co-working pod without a price tag. Not everything meaningful belongs in your business model.

Networking isn't supposed to feel like a game of musical chairs where everyone is rushing to claim the last seat before the music stops. But that's what happens when we're focused on seeking clout, not connection.

When we instead build rooms where the most marginalized feel not just welcomed but safe, that's how we stop treating access as a prize to win.

The point isn't to be in "the right room." It's to make the room right, so no one has to compete for a seat or prove they deserve to stay.

9.

The Productivity Problem

I quit my last corporate job in search of freedom. No more cubicles, no more meetings that should've been emails, and no more forced creativity between 9 am and 5 pm. I was ready to work when and how I wanted.

A few months into self-employment, however, I realized that I hadn't escaped anything. The only difference was that my boss now had my face. She praised my productivity and berated me for "falling short." She compared my performance to others'. She denied my vacation requests. She had sky-high expectations and rock-bottom compassion. The only real difference? The dress code now allowed for pajamas, which was pretty awesome.

I had become the boss I used to resent. The one who rewarded overwork and called it commitment. I may have left Corporate America, but I didn't leave capitalism. I worked as many (or more) hours than I had in an office, but now my self-worth was tied to invoices and inboxes, and I mistook exhaustion for evidence of ambition. Every win demanded a new milestone. I hadn't created freedom. I'd only built a shinier cage.

That's the mind-fuck of hustle culture: it convinces you that you're rebelling when you're only rebranding compliance with capitalism. Being your own boss feels like a freeing goal, but recreating the capitalist hierarchy with yourself at the top isn't freedom at all. Liberation isn't about escaping a boss to become your own. It's about dismantling the system that taught us we ever needed one.

Today, I work at my desk during my designated work hours, then close my laptop when the day is done. I rest without earning it. I don't punish myself for "falling behind," because deadlines can change. I remember that urgency is optional, and that my humanity is not on the clock. My body, not productivity metrics, is now my primary source of truth. That shift didn't happen overnight, and I still have setbacks, but it's changed how every workday feels. The one thing that hasn't changed, however, is the dress code.

How We Learned to Worship Work

If you feel guilty when you're not working, you're fluent in capitalism.

- The Protestant work ethic told us labor was next to godliness.
- Industrial capitalism turned people into production lines.
- Patriarchy forced women to prove they belonged by outworking men.
- White supremacy built an economy on stolen labor while moralizing exhaustion as virtue.

The result lives in our bodies. Knotted stomachs. Headaches that arrive by midafternoon. Jaw clenched even in rest. Waking already tired. Even when no one is watching, the system keeps time inside us. We learn to self-surveil long after the boss, the clock, or the algorithm is gone.

None of this was accidental. Each system trained us to believe that our worth is our productivity, not our personhood. We wear busyness and exhaustion as badges of honor. That's conditioning. "To be colonized is to accept and buy into the lie of our worth being connected to how much we get done," said Tricia Hersey in *Rest is Resistance*.

Our entire lives we're spoon-fed the lie that hard work is always rewarded. Meritocracy is the story that the ruling class tells to keep everyone else grinding and consuming. We focus on self-improvement instead of structural change, convinced that if we hustle harder, we can outrun the inequity baked into the system. "America loves the myth of a meritocracy more than anything else, because it lets us ignore the reality of the impact of bigotry," wrote Mikki Kendall in *Hood Feminism*. Hustle culture individualizes what is actually systemic.

Hustle isn't a habit, it's hypnosis. It weaponizes our fears (of failure, scarcity, irrelevance) until we do the system's job for it. "Cultures of domination rely on the cultivation of fear as a way to ensure obedience," bell hooks wrote in *All About Love*. And obedience often means you've learned to exploit yourself.

<table>
<tr><td rowspan="4">journal
your
journey</td><td>What stories did I inherit about work and worth?</td></tr>
<tr><td>When do I confuse busyness with value?</td></tr>
<tr><td>How does my body respond when I stop?</td></tr>
<tr><td>What would it mean to believe that rest is productive?</td></tr>
</table>

Rest is Resistance

The beginning of the end of my relationship with hustle culture came when my brother died of an overdose when he was 30 years old. Grief shattered every illusion I had about success equalling worthiness. No amount of work would bring my brother back. No amount of revenue could comfort my pain. No accolades would make me feel less alone. Productivity became irrelevant. My body knew this long before my mind could articulate it. Grief made it impossible to pretend that overriding my needs was strength.

Grief exposes every system that teaches you to override your body and abandon your needs. It doesn't care about deadlines or deliverables. It refuses urgency and demands presence. In doing so, it reveals how much of our lives are organized around avoiding stillness rather than honoring what's real.

That's when I began to understand what Tricia Hersey means by her manifesto, *Rest is Resistance*. Honoring our needs is a political stance against a system that would rather extract from us than sustain us. Every slow morning, every unhurried walk, every day spent grieving instead of working is an act of rebellion; a refusal to measure worth by a capitalist yardstick.

Dr. Barbara J. Love provides a roadmap: *awareness → analysis → action → accountability*. Awareness is noticing you're exhausted. Analysis is naming the system that benefits from that exhaustion. Action is saying no. Accountability is not passing the same harm to others. This is how rest becomes a leadership practice, not just a personal coping strategy.

Capitalism treats productivity as proof of worth. Liberation treats aliveness as the measure. The goal isn't to do less for the sake of doing less, it's to stop organizing our lives around extraction, urgency, and fear. When rest, pace, and capacity become central, productivity stops being a moral test and becomes a tool we can choose or refuse. Liberation starts when you awaken to the truth that you're human before you're useful.

Awareness: What stories make rest feel unsafe?

Analysis: Who benefits when I stay tired?

Action: What's one "no" that protects my peace?

Accountability: How can I lead so others can rest too?

Are You Still in the Hustle?

Hustle culture is sneaky; it shapeshifts into *passion*, *drive*, or *commitment*. Let's see where it still lives rent-free in your brain.

- ☐ I feel guilty when I rest, even if I'm exhausted.
- ☐ I treat rest like a reward instead of a requirement.
- ☐ I measure my worth by how much I get done.
- ☐ I call overwhelm "busy" so it sounds impressive.
- ☐ My first instinct when something feels off is to work harder.
- ☐ I feel anxious if I'm not posting, producing, or planning.
- ☐ I've said "after ______, then I'll rest" more than once.
- ☐ I celebrate productivity more than presence.
- ☐ I track my income more closely than my energy.
- ☐ I know my quarterly goals better than my body's needs.
- ☐ I feel more comfortable rushing than being still with myself.

If you checked three or more, welcome to being human inside a system designed to keep you running. Noticing it is the first act of resistance. As Paulo Freire teaches in *Pedagogy of the Oppressed*, developing a critical consciousness through reflection (conscientization) is a cornerstone of liberation.

liberation in action

A CEO client kept promising to give herself more time off, "when ______ happens." But once she reached one milestone, another would appear. Nothing changed.

Our work eventually led to her committing to block out two hours every Friday for herself. No work allowed. She nervously used that time to "indulge" her desires for yoga, naps, and reading.

Slowly, she felt a shift. She felt more clarity, calm, and creativity; less impatience, frustration, and resentment.

That's the paradox of rest: it doesn't steal your edge, it restores your capacity to create without cruelty.

Micro-Liberations

You can't dismantle hustle culture overnight, but you can stop feeding it today.

Schedule rest before work.
At the start of the week, block rest on your calendar first. If something has to move, don't let rest be the default sacrifice.

End the day early.
Choose one day this week to stop working before you feel done. Let regulation, not completion, be the goal.

Audit your brag list.
Notice how often you brag about being productive. Once this week, intentionally praise rest, ease, or presence instead of productivity.

Retire "I'm so busy."
Replace it with "I'm taking my time" or "I'm prioritizing ease." Let the awkwardness be part of the practice.

Let one thing stay unfinished.
Pick something low-stakes and stop before it's complete. Notice that nothing collapses, and how your body softens.

Create a "to-don't" list.
List the tasks, expectations, and obligations you're releasing, those things you only do out of guilt, habit, or fear.

Capitalism keeps us in spreadsheets; liberation lives in the margins. Freedom begins when you stop managing your life like a balance sheet and start remembering that you were never meant to be quantified.

Liberation is a practice. A daily refusal to trade your aliveness for approval. It looks like listening to your body, honoring your limits, and letting enough be enough. It's choosing dignity over discipline and humanity over metrics. That's how you step out of the hustle and into a life that feels like it belongs to you.

If you do only one thing from this chapter, do this:
Ask yourself this question:
If productivity were no longer a measure of worth, what would change?
You don't have to answer yet.
Just notice the discomfort.

10.

Time is a Weapon

Before I became a parent, time felt elastic. I could stretch a morning into a creative sprint, lose an afternoon inside ideas, or take a midweek nap. I didn't think of it as privilege. I thought I "earned" that flexibility because of smart choices and hard work.

Then I had a child. Suddenly, every minute belonged to someone else. My days were filled with care labor, and my nights were filled with guilt for all the work that didn't get done. Only then did I understand that time isn't personal. It's political because access to it is shaped by money, care labor, and safety.

When I was child-free and comfortably upper middle-class, I could trade money for time (order takeout or hire a housecleaner). There are entire industries built to return hours to the privileged. But that calculus only works if you have disposable income to outsource exhaustion. What gets called "good time management" is usually just privilege in disguise. It doesn't just soften the edges; it buys you more hours in the day than everyone else gets.

Motherhood made it undeniable that I didn't have a time-management problem, I had an access problem. The spaciousness I thought I'd earned had always been unevenly distributed. We don't "all have the same 24 hours a day." Most of us start our days in debt to our families, jobs, and systems never designed for our thriving. The debt compounds with each marginalized identity we hold. As a white, educated, able-bodied woman, I will always have more access than many. Even with that privilege, it never feels like enough.

Time isn't equal. It never has been. When we talk about liberation, we have to talk about time because it's the truest determinant of whether we get to live as if we belong to ourselves. For many of us, the cage isn't locked anymore, but we're still rationing our time as if it were, afraid that if we step too far into spaciousness, the door might slam shut again. This chapter reimagines how access to time could look.

The Clock is a Colonial Invention

I've felt rushed since I was 12 years old. I sprinted toward adulthood. By 35, I'd built an impressive résumé—and an unsustainable life.

Our entire concept of time was engineered to serve power. For most of human history, we worked in rhythm with nature, laboring a few hours a day and spending the rest on connection. Time was circular, communal, and abundant. Then came ownership of land, people, and labor. The Agricultural Revolution introduced scarcity; the Industrial Revolution perfected exploitation by standardizing time and turning life into labor.

As Silvia Federici wrote in *Caliban and the Witch*, capitalism required a new sexual division of labor that still shapes our lives today by turning a woman's body into a "machine for the production of new workers," and assigning women unpaid care work. White supremacy enforced the colonization of time by branding Black rest as laziness and Indigenous rhythm as primitive. This "grind culture scam," as Tricia Hersey calls it, is a deliberate inheritance from slavery meant to strip Black and Brown people of humanity.

Time pressure isn't evenly distributed because it was designed not to be, and most of us feel that daily. Urgency has always been a tool of control. We inherit it like a family heirloom we never asked for. It's passed down through homes, workplaces, and classrooms until it feels like our own voice.

Time scarcity doesn't just happen, it's imposed. When certain groups are expected to overwork, over-give, and oversee everyone else's needs, the clock is a weapon. If you always feel behind, it's not a personal flaw. You're living in a system that profits from your hurry. Time was never meant to be neutral. It was invented to discipline bodies and extract labor. The more marginalized your identity, the more hours the system steals. Unlearning that conditioning is holy work. When you pause or slow down, you're resisting a 300-year-old lie.

<table>
<tr><td>journal
your
journey</td><td>What rhythms make me feel most alive?

What would I lose (or gain) if I slowed down?

How might liberation look in my calendar?

Who could benefit if I made slowing down contagious?</td></tr>
</table>

Time Is Collective

Capitalism treats time like private property, as if it's something to hoard, monetize, and control. Liberation reminds us that time doesn't belong to anyone. When we see time as collective, rest stops being a personal indulgence and becomes a communal act. Interdependence helps to redistribute possibility.

This is why your decision to slow down is never just about you. My slower pace gives you permission to breathe, your boundary helps me to protect mine. When one person opts out of urgency, it creates slack in the system. Collective time is built through countless small refusals. Without it, every need becomes an emergency and every pause feels like a failure.

In *Braiding Sweetgrass*, Robin Wall Kimmerer describes time as relational and cyclical. "Time as objective reality has never made much sense to me. It's what happens that matters. How can minutes and years, devices of our own creation, mean the same thing to gnats and to cedars?" Our bodies know this rhythm instinctively; capitalism trains us to ignore it.

There are hierarchies of urgency. The powerful move freely through time, buffered by wealth and safety, while everyone else sprints to keep up.

We reclaim time when we reject the myth of time management and embrace *time stewardship,* a shift from individual optimization to collective care. Stewardship is about refusing to organize life around extraction. It's about moving at a pace that honors your humanity without apology.

After having her second baby in two years, an agency-owner client hit a wall she didn't see coming. Her capacity had changed, but the voice in her head kept insisting her workload shouldn't. She carried the pressure of being the family's primary provider, and the weight of a culture that demands Black women be unbreakable.

We worked to honor her new pace vs. fighting it. She set firmer boundaries, cut offers that drained her, and paused what could wait knowing she could return once daycare started (without treating the break as failure).

Once she stopped punishing herself for having less time, she finally felt like she could breathe inside the time she did have.

Unpacking Time as a Tool of Capitalism

*with **Desireé B. Stephens**, somatic educator, counselor, community builder, and founder of Make Shi(f)t Happen.*

Becky Mollenkamp: When did you realize your relationship to time wasn't only personal, but cultural and political?

Desireé B. Stephens: I was in my 20s, in the middle of a divorce, raising an 11-year-old, and needing to survive without collapsing my body or family in the process. I didn't have the luxury of pretending time was neutral. I had to make money. I had to make school dropoff work. I had to stay present. The standard 9-to-5 model could not hold all of that at once. So I carved a different world.

I took a cleaning job specifically because it allowed me to set my own hours. That choice wasn't about hustle or independence mythology, it was about alignment. It was the first time I understood, viscerally, that the problem wasn't my capacity, discipline, or motivation. The problem was that dominant time structures were never designed for caregiving bodies, for survival, or for healing.

From there, I built my own company so I could continue to navigate time relationally rather than obediently. I haven't used an alarm in over a decade. Not because I don't work, but because my life is organized around responsiveness instead of coercion. I've raised my second set of children this way too, outside of urgency as a default setting. That's when it became clear: what we call "time management" is often just compliance training. And refusing that training was not a personal quirk, it was a political act of care.

Becky: Many cultures understand time as cyclical or relational rather than linear. What does that allow that capitalist time doesn't?

Desireé: Cyclical and relational time allow repair. They allow grief, regeneration, seasons of intensity followed by seasons of rest. They allow knowledge to deepen instead of constantly needing to scale. They allow people to re-learn, re-visit, and remember without shame. Capitalist time shuts that down. Linear time demands constant forward motion, regardless of cost. It treats pauses as failures and repetition as inefficiency. Cyclical time understands that growth isn't a straight line, it spirals. It loops. It composts. That orientation makes room for wisdom, not just output.

Becky: Why did capitalism need to alter our relationship to time?

Desireé: You can't build an economy dependent on endless accumulation if people are oriented toward seasons, community rhythms, or bodily limits. So time had to be severed from land, from ancestry, from the body and standardized. Once time became something you could 'waste,' people could be disciplined through guilt and fear. Once time became money, survival itself became conditional on obedience to the clock. Capitalism didn't just reorganize labor, it reorganized perception.

Becky: How does challenging dominant time norms threaten capitalism?

Desireé: If people stop believing that urgency equals importance, the whole system wobbles. Capitalism relies on people confusing speed with value and exhaustion with worthiness. When you challenge dominant time norms, you expose how much labor is unnecessary, how much urgency is manufactured, and how much harm is normalized. Slowing down threatens profit margins, and more importantly, it threatens control. People who aren't constantly rushed are harder to manipulate. They notice more and ask better questions. They remember.

Becky: You say urgency lives in the calendar *and* the nervous system. How so?

Desireé: Supremacy culture trains the body through threat and reward. Through scarcity. Through surveillance. Through punishment for rest and praise for self-abandonment. Over time, urgency becomes internalized, not as a thought, but as a sensation. Tight chests. Shallow breath. The inability to sit still. The constant feeling of being 'behind' even when nothing is wrong. This is how obedience becomes embodied. You don't need someone standing over you with a stopwatch if your nervous system already believes slowing down is dangerous. Supremacy culture doesn't just teach ideas, it conditions reflexes.

Becky: In a culture obsessed with productivity, how do we resist urgency?

Desireé: Resistance doesn't always look like quitting everything. Sometimes it looks like refusing to rush conversations. Taking a breath before responding. Choosing depth over volume. Letting something take the time it needs instead of the time the system demands. It looks like honoring rest without earning it. Saying no without over-explaining. Designing your life around sustainability instead of optimization. These are small acts, but they're not neutral. When enough people interrupt the training, urgency loses its grip.

- Urgency is capitalism's favorite theft of peace, rest, and attention.

- Every ASAP, quick turnaround, or "circling back" hides a power play.

- You can opt out. Is this urgent or just convenient for someone else?

- True leadership models calm, not chaos.

New Time Metrics

Replace these capitalist yardsticks with liberatory ones:

Instead of measuring...	Try noticing...
Hours worked	Energy sustained
Tasks completed	Moments of presence
Deadlines met	Boundaries honored
Revenue earned	Relief felt
Inbox zero	Nervous system steady

Each metric is a small act of decolonization.

Micro-Liberations

Unfuck your relationship with time, starting with these daily practices.

> **Redefine success in writing.**
> Write a sentence that defines your vision of success *without* money (ease, equity, joy, sustainability). Use it as a check before making decisions.
>
> **Trust your body before your browser.**
> When deciding what to prioritize, ask your body first: Do I feel tight or open? Only after that do you research, optimize, or seek advice.
>
> **Remove one urgency signal.**
> Delete "ASAP," "urgent," or "quick question" from your language this week. Notice what actually breaks (usually nothing).
>
> **Redistribute time.**
> Kill fake urgency. Shorten meetings. Build policies that share time freedom as equity, not privilege.
>
> **Set a default reply window.**
> Add an email autoresponder that says you reply within 24 or 48 hours, and honor it. Clear expectations reduce urgency for you and others.
>
> **Build in a pause.**
> When someone makes an ask, allow an hour to feel into the request before giving an answer. Urgency is often a trauma response, not truth.

Time will keep trying to own you. It will whisper that you're behind, that you should have done more, that you're running out. You're not late to your life, you're living inside a system that profits from making you feel that way. Urgency is a tactic.

Your slowness is a refusal. Every moment you reclaim for rest, joy, care, or nothing at all is resistance. Each pause is a seed, and the more you plant, the more you help propagate a world that moves at the pace of humanity.

If you do only one thing from this chapter, do this:
Choose one place to slow down, even if nothing else changes.
Your pace doesn't just shape your life.
It shapes what becomes possible for others.

11.

The Attention Economy

I've always been desperate to "get my shit together." So much so that I ran an annual roundup of planners on my blog. Every January, I'd crack open a beautiful new paper planner convinced this would be the year I'd finally master my time. And by February, the blank pages would mock me.

Then I started to notice other patterns: I couldn't watch a TV show without also checking my email. I felt a physical itch to immediately clear little red notifications from my iPhone. I couldn't wait 5 minutes after posting on social media before checking for likes.

My attention wasn't just scattered, it was starved. And like any scarcity, it made me easier to control.

I assumed my attention problem was a personal failing, proof that I wasn't trying hard enough. Then in 2020, I watched *The Social Dilemma*, a Netflix documentary about Facebook. Two years later, I read *Stolen Focus* by Johann Hari. Suddenly, things began to click into place: my attention isn't broken, it's being harvested. On purpose, for profit. Every ping, every scroll, every cortisol spike stacks into a constant hum of urgency. And urgency is the oxygen white-supremacist capitalist patriarchy breathes.

Since then, I've made changes. I work only during my actual work hours. I put my laptop in "Do Not Disturb" mode for large chunks of the day. I took up embroidery to have something creative to do with my hands instead of doomscrolling. Some days, it feels revolutionary. But I'm still living inside the attention-stealing machine. Even as I claw back pieces of my focus, the system keeps doing what it was designed to do—keeping me overwhelmed, overstimulated, and too distracted to question harm.

Holding perfect focus isn't a realistic goal. Humans don't work that way. But we can wake up to how our attention is being stolen. This chapter is about how we gently choose (in the ways we each can), to take back our attention.

Your Attention Is Not Neutral

Our attention has never been neutral. Those in power need it. Control attention and you control behavior.

- Clocks and factory bells trained people to surveil their own time.
- Advertising taught us to desire what we didn't need.
- Television perfected the formula: sell attention, not products.
- Then came the internet, social media, and AI to steal and sell our data and our focus at alarming scale and speed.

Each evolution made the extraction quieter, faster, and easier to deny. The technology changed, but the goal stayed the same. Keep people too distracted to notice what's being taken.

As Shoshana Zuboff argues in *The Age of Surveillance Capitalism*, "digital colonialism" treats your attention like a raw material to be mined and sold. And, as always, the powerful control that resource. Capitalism doesn't compete for attention; it decides what you see. Safiya Noble's *Algorithms of Oppression* shows how search engines intentionally reproduce racism and sexism.

The attention economy further reveals the oppressive hierarchy of humanity. Black, Brown, disabled, poor, queer, fat, immigrant, and gender-nonconforming people are expected to give attention while being denied it.

In addition to reinforcing oppression, the attention economy keeps us overwhelmed so we don't organize, resist, and revolt. Worse, we're not only consumed by the machine, we feed it. We endlessly post because we fear being forgotten. We react instantly because momentum feels like survival.

The system doesn't just steal our attention, it trains us to extract attention from each other. We reproduce the very dynamics we resist. We've become both the product and the salesperson. And the more fragmented we become, the easier it is for oppressive systems to operate unnoticed in the background.

<table>
<tr><td rowspan="4">journal
your
journey</td><td>Where does my attention go without my consent?</td></tr>
<tr><td>Who profits when I am distracted?</td></tr>
<tr><td>What becomes possible when I am present?</td></tr>
<tr><td>Where am I feeding the machine out of fear?</td></tr>
</table>

Attention as Sovereignty

Capitalism treats attention as fuel. Something to be captured, redirected, and monetized in service of growth and control. The faster it can move your focus —from outrage to envy to urgency—the more profitable it becomes. In this system, distraction isn't a failure. It's the point. That's why reclaiming attention often feels uncomfortable before it feels freeing.

Liberation reframes attention as sovereignty. Your attention is not infinite, neutral, or disposable. It is how meaning is made. What you give attention to shapes what you believe is possible, what you feel responsible for, and what futures you can imagine. When attention is fragmented, power concentrates elsewhere. When attention is reclaimed, clarity returns.

Attention sovereignty doesn't mean perfect focus or digital purity. It means recognizing that where your attention goes is a political act. Every scroll, click, and reaction either feeds systems built on extraction or interrupts them. Choosing presence over urgency is not disengagement; it's refusal.

When you reclaim your attention, you reclaim your capacity to think critically, feel deeply, and act with intention. You stop reacting to what's loudest and start responding to what matters. That's how attention becomes not just personal protection, but collective possibility. Liberation begins when your attention stops serving capitalism and starts serving your life.

Attention Audit

A 5-minute daily check-in to reveal how your attention is being used.

Morning (1 min.)	→ How does my body feel as I start the day? → What is already competing for my attention? → What do I actually want to pay attention to today?
Mid-day (1 min.)	→ Where has my attention gone so far? → Did my attention wander or was it pulled? → What boundary could help for the next few hours?
Evening (3 mins.)	→ What fed me today? Drained me? → What needs my attention that I've been avoiding? → How can I begin tomorrow with intention?

Unpacking Business Without Social Media

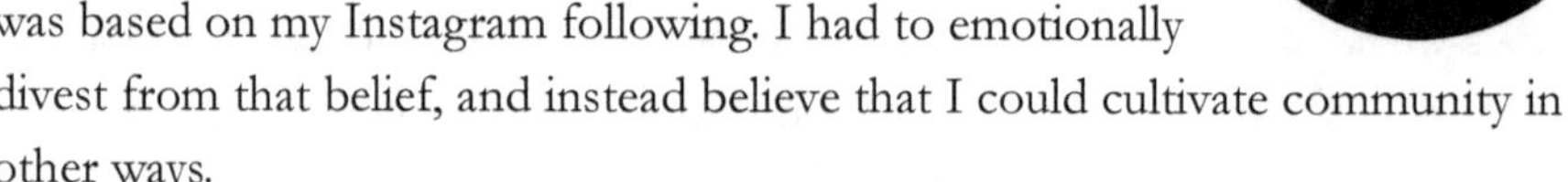

with **Amelia Hruby, PhD**, *author of* Your Attention is Sacred, *who left social media in April of 2021.*

Becky Mollenkamp: Did you have fears about leaving social media?

Amelia Hruby: I had a ton! What if everybody forgets who I am or never invites me to anything? What if I can't make money? I really believed that the success of my work was based on my Instagram following. I had to emotionally divest from that belief, and instead believe that I could cultivate community in other ways.

Becky: How did it feel to step away from social media?

Amelia: It felt anxiety-inducing at first, but I found that I gradually returned to human pace. There are also times when I miss out on things, and I had to deal with those feelings. But I've cultivated new sharing practices, and my work has traveled farther than it ever did on social media.

Becky: What keeps us feeling trapped on social media?

Amelia: The apps know how long it takes for their algorithm to curate the right mix of things to make your brain want more and more, and how to get you to spend money. If you feel like you can't leave social media, it's not your fault. It's designed to be addictive, and I understand how it feels to be caught in that trap.

Becky: Can a business survive off social media?

Amelia: Absolutely. You may have to cultivate different skills. You may have to flex different muscles., but you can have a life and business without being on any of these apps. It's possible if you can open your mind to it.

Becky: What's been the best part of leaving social media for you?

Amelia: My attention returned to the things I actually care about, not the things that everybody else is trying to get me to care about. Leaving social media was both no big deal *and* a radical shift in my attention and my life.

Micro-Liberations

Here are small and doable practices for reclaiming your attention.

Slow your consumption.
Choose three trusted sources for news or information and ignore the rest. If it's important, it will reach you twice.

Post at the speed of integrity.
When you feel the urge to react, share, or respond immediately, challenge yourself to wait 24 hours. If it still feels aligned tomorrow, post it.

Schedule screen-free time daily.
Block one window each day (even 30 minutes) with no phone, no email, no scrolling. Treat it as non-negotiable nervous system care.

Create an attention budget.
Decide in advance where your attention goes today (work, people, rest, learning). When it's spent, stop giving it away.

Define "enough visibility."
Write down what level of online presence feels supportive, not impressive. Once you meet it, log off without guilt.

Reclaim embodied attention.
Once an hour, do a grounding action: stand up, stretch, or take five slow breaths. Attention stabilizes when it has somewhere physical to land.

You don't have to delete every app or disappear from the internet. Liberation doesn't require silence (quite the contrary), but it does require sovereignty.

When you choose where your attention goes, you reclaim your ability to think clearly, feel deeply, create intentionally, rest unapologetically, and imagine boldly. Your attention is not a resource for capitalism to exploit. It is the foundation of your liberation. Protect it like your future depends on it, because it does.

If you do only one thing from this chapter, do this:
Reclaim a small pocket of your attention from a system designed to steal it.
What you attend to becomes your world, so choose carefully.

Interlude

Words Create Worlds

The dominant culture uses language as a tool of hierarchy. If we don't interrogate the words we inherit, we end up living inside someone else's worldview. This mini-dictionary presents typical oppressive vocabulary used in business, alongside reframed, liberatory definitions. Pay attention to which version of each word you're living, selling, or rewarding. Language doesn't just describe our businesses; it builds them.

Oppressive Definition

Liberatory Definition

Accountability

A form of punishment used to correct, control, or discipline individuals for missteps or failures.

A practice of repair, responsibility, and alignment that strengthens relationships and deepens trust within a community.

Access

Something granted to those who can pay, network, or leverage privilege to get beyond the gate.

The collective responsibility to ensure that participation is not determined by wealth or status.

Ambition

The relentless pursuit of more (money, growth, output, recognition), regardless of personal cost.

The desire to pursue meaningful goals with care, integrity, and regard for your humanity and the humanity of others.

Authenticity

A branding tactic used to appear relatable while still maximizing influence and sales.

Showing up as yourself without erasure, grounded in safety and consent.

Authority

The right to dominate or speak above others, rooted in hierarchy, confidence, and perceived expertise.

The responsibility to contribute within community, grounded in accountability, lineage, and shared power.

Oppressive Definition

Liberatory Definition

Brand

A polished persona created to persuade audiences and differentiate oneself in the marketplace.

A clear expression of values, commitments, and relationships that signal who you are in community.

Boundaries

Rigid rules used to control people or optimize personal efficiency and productivity.

Relational commitments that protect your well-being and honor the capacity and dignity of everyone involved.

Capacity

How much work you can produce within a limited time.

A dynamic state shaped by energy, care, and circumstance.

Care

A customer service strategy intended to increase loyalty, retention, and profit.

The shared practice of meeting needs with compassion, presence, and respect.

Collaboration

A tactical partnership designed to expand reach, visibility, or revenue.

A reciprocal relationship that nurtures trust, creativity, and collective wisdom.

Community

An audience cultivated to extract attention, engagement, and future sales.

A collective of people connected by care, reciprocity, and shared values.

Credibility

Earned by performing certainty and presenting a polished image.

Earned through integrity, transparency, and aligned action.

Expertise

The accumulation of credentials, achievements, and authority that place one above others.

A combination of lived experience, learning, and perspective that grows through community and practice.

Oppressive Definition   Liberatory Definition

Framework

A proprietary system branded as original to position someone as an expert or innovator.

One contribution in an ongoing conversation, rooted in lineage and shared with proper attribution.

Growth

Continuous expansion of output and revenue, regardless of human impact.

Intentional deepening of alignment and capacity within humane limits.

Impact

Measured by scale, reach, and numbers that demonstrate market dominance.

Measured by depth, resonance, and meaningful change within communities.

Influence

The ability to persuade or shape behavior to achieve personal or financial gain.

Shared power to inspire collective action and support community transformation.

Integrity

A personal brand attribute used to signal trustworthiness without structural accountability.

The ongoing commitment to align your actions with your values, even when it requires repair or discomfort.

Knowledge

Intellectual property to package, trademark, or monetize for competitive gain.

A shared resource that grows through lineage, experience, and collaboration.

Leadership

The ability to control or influence people from a position of authority.

The practice of stewarding collective power so all can thrive.

Marketing

The art of persuasion used to generate desire, urgency, and sales.

The practice of sharing information with clarity, consent, and respect.

Oppressive Definition	Liberatory Definition
Mentorship A hierarchical relationship where wisdom flows downward from expert to novice.	A reciprocal exchange where everyone teaches, learns, and grows together.
Power The ability to dominate, direct, or control others to achieve personal objectives.	Acting collectively and redistributing resources in order to expand liberation.
Productivity The measure of a person's worth based on how much they produce.	A rhythm shaped by capacity, seasons, and the need for rest and repair.
Recognition The selective reward given to the loudest, most visible, or most privileged voices.	A collective practice of acknowledging contributions from all involved.
Resilience The expectation that individuals should endure harm without support.	The communal ability to navigate difficulty with care and solidarity.
Rest A luxury that must be earned by meeting productivity goals.	A non-negotiable need that fuels healing, creativity, and sustainable change.
Safety The absence of visible harm.	Conditions that support full humanity.
Success The achievement of wealth, prestige, visibility, and external validation.	A life aligned with your values, capacity, and well-being.
Sustainability A business strategy used to increase longevity and profitability.	The practice of honoring limits, protecting resources, and choosing what can be maintained without harm.

Section 3

The Business We're Told to Build

By the time we start a business, most of us have already absorbed the rules of the game. We're told to scale, optimize, capture attention, become a thought leader, perform authenticity, hack the algorithm, build an empire.

This section dismantles all of that. Here, we explore how the dominant business playbook was designed inside white-supremacist capitalist patriarchy, and why so much of it feels like self-abandonment. We'll look at the stories baked into our language, the harm built into traditional sales systems, the surveillance disguised as strategy, and the way "professionalism" quietly replicates oppression.

Most importantly, this section names what many entrepreneurs feel but rarely say out loud: You don't have to build a business that harms you to succeed or to be taken seriously. These chapters are a wrecking ball to the performative, extractive models we inherited. But they're also an invitation: to build something more human, more relational, and more liberatory.

This section isn't about swapping tactics. It's about unlearning the logic beneath them. It's where we stop performing business and start reimagining it.

From here on, we stop diagnosing the system and start choosing differently.

12.

F*ck Funnels

After leaving freelance writing, I moved into online business coaching. In those early years, I spent far too much time trying to build the "perfect funnel," a system that would bring in money while I slept.

I downloaded every "proven high-converting" email sequence freebie, bought more $79 courses than I care to admit, and paid $10,000 to a business coach and a marketing strategist. Over time, I loaded my website with opt-ins, tripwires, timers, bonuses, and upsells. I spent endless hours every week creating content for my blog, newsletter, and every social media platform. Despite what the experts promised, I didn't end up making millions in "passive" income or having an automated pipeline of perfect-fit clients. Instead, I added a massive amount of unpaid labor to my plate. What I earned was exhaustion and a feeling that my work was no longer mine.

At some point, I paused and thought about how I'd built my first successful business years earlier, before funnels were packaged and sold online. Back then, I wasn't treating strangers like leads. I spent time in communities, invited people into conversations, and built relationships. In short, I'd been running the sort of human-first business that had always existed.

What finally broke the spell wasn't strategy fatigue, but the realization that funnels require us to relate to people as metrics instead of humans. The problem wasn't that I was doing funnels wrong. It was that I was being asked to override my values to make a system work.

Funnels promised efficiency, but what they actually demanded was distance. They rewarded urgency over care, manipulation over consent, and volume over relationship. The more closely I followed the rules, the less recognizable my work became to me and to the people I serve. I started to feel like success required a version of myself I didn't want to keep performing.

This chapter explores how marketing looks when relationships are priority.

Marketing as Manipulation

The traditional marketing playbook is lifted straight from white-supremacist capitalist patriarchy. The same tools of oppression are mirrored in the ways we're told to sell and scale. Scarcity, secrecy, and speed aren't marketing best practices; they're tools of manipulation, control, and extraction.

- False scarcity teaches people to override their needs and resources.
- Manufactured urgency weaponizes anxiety, and punishes deliberation, disability, and trauma pacing.
- Opaque pricing and punitive payment plans reward only the seller.
- Privilege dressed up as authority replicates oppressive hierarchy.

These practices don't just sell offers; they reproduce power. They teach people who gets to decide, who must comply, and who absorbs the risk. Over time, they train both sellers and buyers to mistake coercion for choice.

Feminist marketer Kelly Diels' work on consent-based, culture-making marketing asks us to treat every tactic as political—because it is. Ask: "Does this build agreement or engineer pressure?"

In *The Antiracist Business Book*, Trudi Lebron says marketing and sales that don't center racial equity protect the status quo, no matter your intentions. "It's really easy to fall into oppressive, manipulative, misaligned tactics in our sales and marketing process, because...many entrepreneurs are so focused on scaling that we forget to apply our equity lens to this aspect of our business."

Inclusive marketing strategist Sonia Thompson says good marketing starts with deeply understanding who we serve and designing every touchpoint so they feel seen, respected, and safe. Desiree Adaway's anti-oppressive work adds that we must move from transactional to transformational relationships.

Their work asks us to review marketing through an equity and consent lens, and to treat each launch as a chance to practice the future we're building.

<table>
<tr><td rowspan="4">journal
your
journey</td><td>Where am I manufacturing urgency I don't really have?</td></tr>
<tr><td>If I trusted my audience, what would I stop doing?</td></tr>
<tr><td>How would marketing look if my main KPI was trust?</td></tr>
<tr><td>How would it feel to sell at the speed of consent?</td></tr>
</table>

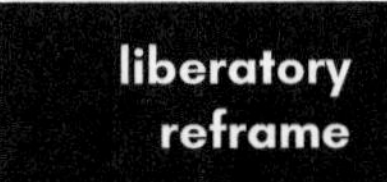

Consent-Based Marketing

Consent-based marketing treats people as sovereign decision-makers, not leads to be converted. Feminist marketing pro Kelly Diels teaches that oppressive marketing relies on psychological exploitation because capitalism assumes people can't be trusted to choose for themselves. Consent-based marketing rejects that lie. It assumes adults are capable of discernment.

Liberatory marketing is spacious. It isn't a formula, but a way of relating. It assumes people deserve clarity, time, and autonomy. It moves at the speed of trust, not the speed of extraction. What it looks like in practice:

Informed consent: Tell people what they need to know before they need to know it, from pricing to expectations to risks. No bait and switch.

No coercion: Skip countdown timers, FOMO, and shame-based scripts about "playing small," "not investing in yourself," or "missing your chance."

Transparent limits: Swap "only one spot left," for "I can serve 12 people."

Built-in access: Captions, transcripts, clear readability, sensory-friendly pacing, and asynchronous access.

Relational metrics: Measure care more than clicks. Re-enrollment, referrals, replies, and unsolicited praise tell you more than open rates ever will.

When marketing honors autonomy, people feel respected, and safer to say "yes" or "no." A business that can withstand "no" is one built on integrity, not manipulation. Consent-based marketing isn't the loudest strategy, but it is the most credible, sustainable, and humane.

Information offered plainly, not buried or baited. The ability to ask questions without consequence. Time and space to listen to their bodies, resources, and instincts without pressure. If these conditions aren't present, consent isn't either.

Unpacking Feminist Marketing

*with **Kelly Diels**, a feminist marketing consultant who challenges exploitation baked into sales culture.*

Becky Mollenkamp: How is shame used in marketing?

Kelly Diels: It's literally the fundamental principle of most copywriting systems: Find a problem, agitate it, induce a lot of shame in your clients, and they'll buy to get out of that emotional state. That will land hardest on people who've been traumatized and abused, who are marginalized and have experienced bias against their identity and had resources systemically withheld for generations or presently. I don't think it's okay to leverage oppression and pain to profit. That's not a function of flourishing, and it's not a world I want to live in. I've experienced far too much of that in my life, and I'm not going to inflict that on other people when there are other—better—ways of doing it.

Becky: You engaged in toxic marketing when you started. What changed?

Kelly: I'd execute those tactics for about 3 months, then collapse, and then I'd build myself back up, do it again, and collapse again. I couldn't sustain it. The friction between my principles and what I was required to do was too high. Eventually, I started writing about the 'Female Lifestyle Empower Brand' and how it leverages white, thin, beauty, class, and youth privileges to build businesses. But what if those tactics aren't available to us or are morally reprehensible to us? I thought, 'there's a political issue, so I'm going to tell the truth, and figure out how to build different systems for myself.' Once I started figuring them out for myself, I started teaching them to other people.

Becky: What works if you don't want to use oppressive marketing?

Kelly: Sometimes it's easiest to figure out what you hate and do the opposite. See what works and build a system. That's a good way to start generating your own practices and trusting your instincts as an entrepreneur. Some of it will fail, but that's okay. I approach my business like a science experiment. Did it work? No, stop doing it. Did it work? Great, let's do more of it. As an example, I hated blame-y, shame-y sales pages, so I decided to try writing a sales letter that was a love letter to my clients. It worked and I still do it.

Becky: You believe in consent in marketing. Why, and how do you do it?

Kelly: I had a pretty formative experience of what it feels like to not have your consent be valued. It's central to my existence that we get consent, and it's not one and done. Just because someone signs up to my email list doesn't mean they consent to hear every single thing that I want to send for the rest of time. I send an email at the start of every launch giving people a link to unsubscribe to the sales emails. The first time I did that, I thought everyone would opt out. But an extraordinary thing happened. One person said the email confirmed that I was the right teacher for her and bought a more expensive program. Many people thanked me for the email. I expected to fail and was surprised by winning.

Becky: You believe marketing can be a tool for liberation. How so?

Kelly: I think every human on Earth is a culture maker. If we all died tomorrow, all of our cultures would die, too. We are the vehicles by which culture flows, and we can do it deliberately. I can make a decision to interrupt patterns that I object to and amplify those I want to support. We can also critically examine the ways we grow our businesses and ask, 'how can this also grow a culture that I feel comfortable in, that the people that I love feel comfortable in, and that everybody and every identity can flourish?' For example, when we're promoting our businesses we can produce media that show a variety of body sizes, shapes, and diversity. We can facilitate a culture in which everyone is welcome.

Becky: Is it possible to practice liberatory marketing *and* make money?

Kelly: Being committed to justice and a world in which we all flourish doesn't mean you're not going to be successful in business. It actually *grew* my business because I attracted the people who shared my principles. It's also totally sustainable because I don't have to manufacture it. Your principles are an ever-renewable, sustainable source of fuel. Being true to what you believe in, and building a business around those things, is what makes business work.

Becky: Shifting how you market your business is difficult. Why is it worth it?

Kelly: It can be grueling to confront your complicity in systems that you may not have known existed. The state of the world, and your role in it—because we're all both oppressors and the oppressed—can make you feel grief-stricken and shame-filled. Even so, this work is worth it. Being able to contribute to a world that you can actually be proud of is worth it. *You* are worth it.

Capitalist Red Flags

If you use any of these tactics, you may be slipping into bro-marketing territory.
- ⚑ "Only 24 hours left!" (but the cart mysteriously reopens next week)
- ⚑ Tripwires that prey on shame or scarcity trauma.
- ⚑ High-ticket = high integrity logic that collapses price with worthiness.
- ⚑ "I manifested a 7-figure month on a beach in Bali" origin stories.
- ⚑ Pain-point poking designed to make people feel broken so they'll buy.
- ⚑ Weaponized vulnerability: oversharing trauma as a sales strategy.
- ⚑ Fake community engagement that's basically a warm-up act for a pitch.
- ⚑ Programs with zero support marketed as self-paced for convenience.
- ⚑ False reciprocity: "I gave you value, now you owe me a sale."
- ⚑ Guilt-inducing opt-outs (*I don't want more money* on the unsubscribe button).
- ⚑ Urgency as empowerment: "Make a bold move today or stay stuck!"

Why Funnels Fail

- ✔ Your lead magnet overpromised and under-delivered.
- ✔ You built the funnel before you built the relationship.
- ✔ You're talking at (not to) people.
- ✔ The offer requires urgency instead of clarity to make sense.
- ✔ You're ignoring economic realities, asking people to stretch past capacity.
- ✔ People feel pressured rather than supported.
- ✔ You're not solving the problem people actually have.
- ✔ People can't (or don't feel safe enough to) ask questions.

True Offer Cost

Hours spent creating offer: ____________

Hours spent managing process: ______

Hours spent creating marketing content: ____________

Money spent on courses, templates, tech, etc.: ____________

Advertising spend: ____________

Actual ROI (*be honest*): ____________

What might look different if those resources went to building relationships?

Micro-Liberations

Small practices to help you market through consent, clarity, and trust.

Replace capture with clarity.
Create a one-page offer that includes who it is and isn't for, timeline, price, and expectations. This gives people what they need to consent.

Name real limits.
If your program can hold 12 people well, say 12. If it's unlimited, say that. Honesty about capacity builds trust.

Trade FOMO for fit.
Add one sentence to your offer that helps people opt out (e.g., "This isn't for you if…"). Fewer wrong yeses = more aligned work.

Price with integrity.
Publish your pricing, offer refunds or trials if possible, and consider equitable pricing so a buyer can choose with dignity.

Make opt-out frictionless.
Check your unsubscribe and opt-out paths. If it takes more than one click to leave, simplify it. Respect builds trust faster than retention tricks.

Invite conversation.
When you extend real guidance (not a sales pitch disguised as service), you become a trusted resource.

If you use oppressive tactics to grow your business, you grow an oppressive business. When you choose consent over coercion, you build a liberated business that people can trust. And businesses built on trust sell better because people feel respected, not pressured. Relational businesses last longer because they weather algorithm swings.

In a world shouting "capture, convert, close," you can choose something different. You can choose to market like a human, and that is revolution.

If you do only one thing from this chapter, do this:
Relate to the next person you market to as a human, not a metric.

13.

F*ck Algorithms, Too

For too long, I played the visibility game. Be everywhere, do everything, don't let the algorithm forget you for even a second. I scattered myself across every platform, as if being in all the places was a sign of my ambition and not evidence of my pressure to perform. The more I contorted myself to fit into every format, the less I recognized myself. I was dancing and lip syncing my way to total embarrassment and exhaustion.

The visibility game didn't ask who I was, but what I could feed it. And it was never satisfied. Something had to change, so I stopped performing and chose alignment. I have two degrees in journalism and spent nearly 20 years as a professional reporter and editor. My preferred communication style is storytelling and the sort of messy nuance that can't be squeezed into a 30-second video. I finally admitted to myself that I wasn't going to lip-sync my way to liberation. I stopped trying to be everywhere and stuck to platforms where I feel the most like myself. To my surprise, my visibility didn't shrink. In fact, my overall reach grew.

The biggest shift came when I stopped chasing the algorithm altogether and started investing in people. My most meaningful visibility has never come from social media, but from the rooms I'm *not* in, from someone saying, "You need to meet Becky." That happens more and more frequently because I approach visibility relationally, not transactionally. I uplift other people's work, I make introductions, and I don't gatekeep. Relational visibility is built through trust (not tricks), and it quietly compounds.

It's important to note that I can do all of that because I carry privilege, which gives me a great deal of safety to be visible. Safety turns visibility from a risk into a responsibility, which changes how I show up.

In this chapter, we'll examine who algorithms reward and punish, and how you can choose more humane ways to be seen.

Visibility Isn't Safety

We're fed the lie that visibility equals relevance. But who gets seen is shaped by algorithms that aren't meritocratic. "Algorithmic oppression is not just a glitch in the system but, rather, is fundamental to the operating system of the web," writes Safiya Noble in *Algorithms of Oppression.*

In other words, the game is rigged before you even log in. Some people are recognized as authorities before they open their mouths, while others work twice as hard to get noticed at all. This isn't about hurt feelings. It's about who gets access to opportunity, safety, and sustainability.

This under-recognition, says brand scientist N. Chloé Nwangwu, is due to the Invisibility Tax, which includes:

- *Reciprocity Ransom:* People with marginalized identities must meet a higher threshold to activate a willingness to reciprocate.
- *Validation Paradox:* Being invited into decision-making spaces but with little real influence or authority.
- *Ambition Penalty:* Marginalized folks hold back to avoid being penalized for displaying confidence, says Stefanie O'Connell Rodriguez.
- *Competence Tax:* Marginalized people, especially Black women, must consistently over-perform and self-police to be perceived as competent, yet that labor rarely translates into visibility.

Also, online platforms expose the least powerful to misrepresentation, harassment, and violence. For women, queer or disabled folks, and people of the global majority, being seen online includes a very real safety calculation—one that often comes with bodily, emotional, and economic risk.

Visibility isn't proof of value, and obscurity is not evidence of failure. When we confuse being seen with being worthy, we allow unjust systems to decide whose work matters, instead of building our own measures of impact and care.

<table>
<tr><td rowspan="4">journal
your
journey</td><td>What would visibility look like if it wasn't exhausting?</td></tr>
<tr><td>Who am I performing for when I post?</td></tr>
<tr><td>How can I show up online in ways that feel sustainable?</td></tr>
<tr><td>What could I create if every idea wasn't 'content'?</td></tr>
</table>

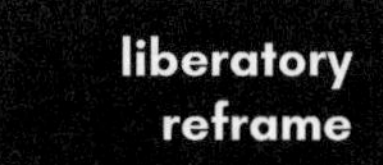

Ecosystem of Influence

The problem was never your ambition, clarity, or output. The problem is a landscape where some people are automatically treated as A-listers and others are relegated to background players, no matter the quality of their work. Algorithms don't just reflect power; they reproduce it.

Liberation isn't chasing visibility inside that system. It's building your own ecosystem of influence that, as N. Chloé Nwangwu says, becomes "impossible to ignore" because it's rooted in recognition, not reach.

Start with your platform: What is your North Star? Develop a clear, sharp articulation of what you stand for and why your work exists. Anchor your presence so people know what they're saying yes to.

Build your circle of recognition: This isn't a networking list or your follower count. It's the people who see you, believe in you, share your work out of alignment, and carry your ideas into rooms you're not in. For marginalized folks, this circle is a counterweight to systemic under-recognition. For privileged folks, it offers a way to redistribute attention rather than hoarding influence.

Design visibility opportunities: Don't depend on algorithmic amplification. Build visibility that is slow, relational, steady, and consent-based. This looks like pitching collaborations that align with your values, hosting intimate conversations instead of chasing mass audiences, and prioritizing safety and community over reach.

Stop performing for platforms: If the algorithm won't recognize your authority, engineer recognition elsewhere (your website, newsletter, community, partnerships, clients). This is visibility that's actually *yours*.

Build for how you want to be treated: Nwangwu says visibility is about setting expectations, boundaries, and norms. Who gets close? What's off-limits? What do you expect from your audience? This protection allows under-recognized people to stay whole while being seen.

This kind of visibility creates conditions where people can stay visible without self-betrayal or constant performance. Liberation is not about getting louder. It's about building an ecosystem that doesn't treat you like background noise, and trains others to refuse it too.

Visibility vs. Recognition

Visibility is what platforms measure. Recognition is what humans respond to. One keeps you posting. The other keeps you in business.

Visibility	Recognition
Follower count	Credibility
Reach	Authority
Impressions	Trust
Algorithmic boosts	Community amplification
Virality	Introductions

Questions to Ask Before Chasing Visibility

Before pouring more time, energy, or money into "getting seen," ask:

- ☐ Is this aligned with my values, or just my ego?
- ☐ Is this attention I actually want or that I'm conditioned to want?
- ☐ Am I creating from desire, or from fear of being forgotten?
- ☐ Is this my voice, or the voice the algorithm rewards?
- ☐ Is visibility safe for me? Or will it cost me something I can't afford?
- ☐ Would any part of me need to shrink, soften, or sanitize to succeed?
- ☐ Am I showing up or performing?
- ☐ Do I feel more powerful in this space or more depleted by it?
- ☐ What would recognition, not visibility, look like for me?
- ☐ What do I think visibility will fix? Is that actually true?
- ☐ Will this visibility expand my impact or just my workload?
- ☐ What boundaries do I need to hold to stay whole while being seen?

Being heard matters more than being seen.

Micro-Liberations

Reclaim your voice, pace, and humanity from the capitalist machine.

Post on your own timeline.
Decide before you create how often you'll share (once a week, twice a month, etc.). If the algorithm wants more, let it want.

Skip the performance.
When writing or recording, picture one real human you care about. If it wouldn't make sense to say it to them, don't post it.

Refuse contortion.
Before following a trend, ask: "What would I have to give up to do this?" If the answer is clarity, dignity, or safety, skip it.

Curate your consumption.
Once a week, mute or unfollow one account that spikes urgency, comparison, or despair. Your nervous system sets the rules, not the feed.

Build on an "owned" channel.
Choose one place you control (newsletter, website, community) and prioritize it over social media platforms.

Choose your own metrics.
Pick 2-3 non-algorithmic signals to track (replies, conversations, referrals, feeling energized). If those are present, visibility is working.

You don't exist to feed an algorithm, especially one designed to convert attention into profit for corporations. When you stop performing for the machine, you reclaim your relationship with your community.

The people meant for you don't need you to be everywhere or always on. They need you to be you, at a pace your body can hold and your spirit can sustain. Freed from constant performance, you realize visibility was never the point. You can stop chasing relevance and start cultivating resonance.

If you do only one thing from this chapter, do this:
Invest in one relationship that exists entirely outside a platform.

14.

The Authenticity Machine

I used to believe that my credibility as a business owner depended on people believing that I had my shit together. Then I had a baby. Running a business while raising a child was like being body-checked by reality. I was tired, lonely, and overwhelmed. All of that despite having an equal partner, family support, and a flexible schedule—privileges so many others don't have in a system that doesn't support new parents. Even with the sleepless nights, fluctuating hormones, and full-time breastfeeding job, I continued to perform "expert energy" because that's what I thought running a successful business required.

On a lark one morning, I completed a "life map," a tool I use with clients. It hit me like a freight train: I was unsatisfied in most areas of my life, especially a lack of friendships. Business and baby had swallowed my time, attention, and emotional bandwidth. On impulse, I hit "live" inside my Facebook group of about 1,000 people and talked about it. When I cried, I was mortified. I'd been trained to believe that authority meant composure, and that composure meant concealment. I wasn't just risking judgment, I feared that I was risking being seen as less serious, less capable, less professional. What if showing too much messiness would cost me my credibility, or my business altogether?

But people didn't laugh or leave, they leaned in. They told me the moment felt honest. Some said it helped them trust me. Looking back, that video didn't matter because I cried. It mattered because I told the truth, and I could tell the truth because I had enough safety to survive it. Not everyone does.

That moment taught me that authenticity alone doesn't create trust. I could be honest because I had enough stability, privilege, and community to absorb any financial, reputational, or relational consequences. That type of safety is a luxury many people don't have. For some, vulnerability is a risk with real consequences. The real question isn't "Why aren't people being more authentic?" but "What would it take for honesty to be safe for everyone?"

The Cost of 'Being Real'

"Pull back the curtain," "speak your truth," and "be yourself" sound like helpful advice, but in a world shaped by oppression, authenticity carries different stakes for people of different identities. What looks like freedom for some functions as a risk assessment for others. Before anyone speaks honestly, the system has already decided how much truth it will tolerate from their body.

Black women, in particular, live on what Ericka Hines, the founder of Black Women Thriving, calls "the tightrope of excellence." They're held to higher standards, allowed fewer mistakes, and punished more severely for deviation. As Kimberlé Crenshaw's work on intersectionality shows, identity is compounding. A queer Black woman doesn't navigate the same authenticity landscape as an immigrant trans man. Who gets to be real depends on who the system protects.

Vulnerability from white leaders is read as relatable or brave, while the same from Black and Brown leaders may be seen as unprofessional, weak, or proof that they can't handle leadership. Authenticity isn't equally safe. Hines' research shows that Black women report feeling pressure to code-switch, downshift their brilliance, mute their emotions, and manage how they're perceived.

The problem isn't that people are afraid to be authentic. It's that the system punishes authenticity unevenly. Without safety and structural support, authenticity isn't empowerment, it's exposure. What gets framed as courage for some becomes a liability for others. The cost of honesty is not evenly distributed. Pretending otherwise protects the system, not the people inside it.

The business world loves camera-ready authenticity from those in the dominant culture because it looks radical without requiring redistribution. The risk stays individualized, while platforms, audiences, and companies reap the rewards of vulnerability they don't have to hold. When authenticity is extracted without care, it becomes just another unpaid form of labor.

<table>
<tr><td rowspan="4">journal
your
journey</td><td>What parts of myself feel safe to share publicly?</td></tr>
<tr><td>What parts of myself require privacy or protection?</td></tr>
<tr><td>Where am I oversharing from pressure, not choice?</td></tr>
<tr><td>Where am I undersharing from fear, not discernment?</td></tr>
</table>

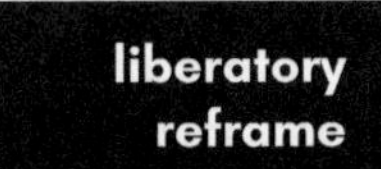

Authenticity to Alignment

Forget being "more real." Liberation refuses the idea that your truth must be public to be authentic. Authenticity isn't just offering yourself up for public consumption. It's building a life and business where you no longer have to negotiate with yourself about which version of you is allowed to show up.

Ericka Hines' research shows that authenticity only flourishes when the environment supports it and people feel psychologically safe. It's not forcing vulnerability, but creating the conditions for it to exist without penalty. When honesty costs too much, people hide parts of themselves to survive.

Reclaiming authenticity starts by reclaiming your relationship to yourself. Not the curated you, but the you who knows what's true beneath the act. Ask: Who am I when I'm not being watched, not performing competence, not optimizing for public consumption? What parts of me have only existed in private because the world wasn't safe enough?

Authenticity is agency over your inner life, not access to it for others. This is an invitation to practice honesty, with yourself first and then with others, without abandoning your boundaries or betraying your safety. Share in ways that strengthen you, and choose when and how you want to be seen. You can be authentic and still allow some things to remain sacred.

It's also important to build systems, inside your business and around your life, that don't require you to be a flattened, optimized version of yourself to succeed. Systems where your pace, capacity, and wellbeing matters. Shift away from authenticity as a marketing tool and toward authenticity as belonging, first to yourself and then to communities that value your safety.

Liberatory authenticity isn't about performing realness. It's about creating a world, starting with your own, where you don't have to perform at all.

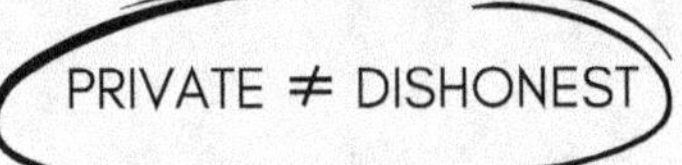

You don't owe the world your inner life. Withholding what isn't safe to share is discernment, not deception. Some truths are meant to be lived, not turned into content.

The Performance Checklist

Are you being authentic or performing a version of yourself the system likes?
Performance often disguises itself as professionalism. This checklist can help
you notice when authenticity has slipped into survival.

- ☐ I'm sharing this for me, not for validation.
- ☐ I'm sharing my truth, not performing for the algorithm.
- ☐ I feel safe sharing this because I trust the people receiving it.
- ☐ I'm choosing this, not reacting to pressure.
- ☐ This comes from alignment, not urgency.
- ☐ I'm not asking the internet to hold what only my community can hold.
- ☐ This honors my nervous system.
- ☐ This feels empowering, not extractive.

Authenticity Without Apology

Here are a few mantras for when you feel pressured to perform:
- ✓ "This is who I am right now."
- ✓ "I'm allowed to change."
- ✓ "I don't need to prove my humanity."
- ✓ "I set the terms of my own visibility."
- ✓ "I get to take up space without justification."
- ✓ "I don't have to show everything to be real."
- ✓ "My boundaries are part of my authenticity."
- ✓ "I can choose what's mine to hold and mine to share."
- ✓ "I'm not here to perform. I'm here to live."

You Don't Owe...
the internet your healing, your audience your pain, anyone
access to your interior life, or constant relatability to be worthy
of connection. Authenticity includes the right to remain whole.

Micro-Liberations

Tiny rebellions to make authenticity without extraction possible.

Define your off-the-record zones.
Write a list of what you'll never share publicly (relationships, your child, money, grief, healing). This list is a boundary, not a lack of authenticity.

Create a private truth outlet.
Choose one place where you can be fully unfiltered (journal, therapist, friend, voice memo). Public platforms don't have to hold that weight.

Process, then translate.
Journal, voice note, or talk it out privately first. Only share what feels settled in your body, not what's still bleeding.

Let your body call the shots.
Check in physically before being "real" in public. Tight chest, shaky hands, urge to overshare = pause. Calm, grounded, spacious = proceed.

Audit your "authenticity ROI."
After each vulnerable post, ask: "Did that create connection or depletion?" If it costs your peace, it's extraction not authenticity.

Practice private joy.
Choose one thing this week that will stay completely undocumented. No posts, no texts, no proof. Let it belong only to you.

The business world has reduced "authenticity" to a slogan. In truth, authenticity is refusing to perform the version of yourself the system prefers. And as Ericka Hines reminds us, it's not something to which we all have equal access.

Stop focusing on "being real" online, and instead put effort into building a world, starting with your corner of it, where truth doesn't cost belonging. The goal has never been to look like you have it all together, but to build a business (and a life) where you don't have to pretend.

If you do only one thing from this chapter, do this:
Stop sharing something publicly just because you feel you "should."
You don't owe anyone access to your inner life.

15.

The Credibility Hustle

When I shifted into coaching in the mid-2010s, the prevailing wisdom was clear: your work wasn't sellable or "scalable" unless you wrapped it in a signature method. Preferably something with three steps, a clever acronym, and a trademark symbol (The Capitalist System**TM**).

I produced my share of half-baked frameworks with alliterative names, borrowed concepts dressed up as original insight, and systems that sounded authoritative but felt hollow when I tried to use them. The harder I worked to sound like an expert, the further I drifted from what made my work useful.

I didn't have language for it at the time, but I was deep in what I now know as the Credibility Hustle. I was operating inside an ecosystem that rewards certainty, hot takes, and ownership, while quietly punishing citation, collaboration, and humility. Credibility was treated like a scarce resource, something you had to claim before someone else did.

Opting out felt risky. If I didn't present myself as the authority, would anyone listen? Would my work be taken seriously? For a long time, that fear kept me performing expertise instead of practicing it. I worried more about visibility than being aligned with my values.

I watched peers build audiences by sounding certain about things that were anything but certain. Nuance didn't travel as far as confidence, and questions didn't convert the way declarations did. The pressure wasn't just to be knowledgeable, but to appear finished. Curiosity felt like a liability, and doubt was something to hide.

What eventually became impossible to ignore was how bad it felt. Not just exhausting, but alienating. The more I chased credibility, the less connected I felt to my values, peers, and the people I was serving. That tension is where the Credibility Hustle does its most effective work. It has to abandon relationship in exchange for recognition. This is where we start refusing that trade.

Rewarding Erasure

We're told that to level up in business, we must become *the* authority, the "thought leader" everyone else in your industry quotes. This is the Credibility Hustle. It rewards hierarchy, individualism, and intellectual hoarding. It demands you market yourself as the genius and the innovator, even when your ideas were shaped or built by thinkers who came before you.

The Credibility Hustle trains us to claim originality, even when it requires erasure. Collaboration becomes a liability and humility a weakness. The result is a culture where sounding smart matters more than being accountable for our impact. This hustle distorts who is allowed to speak. Those closest to power are rewarded for confidence, while those closest to the consequences of harm are dismissed as too emotional or too biased to be credible. Lived experience is mined for insight and then stripped of authorship.

"Knowledge without wisdom is adequate for the powerful, but wisdom is essential to the survival of the subordinate," Patricia Hill Collins wrote in *Black Feminist Thought*. Traditional authority models steal knowledge from the people who lived it and hand the microphone to those with enough distance and privilege to make it sound palatable to dominant culture. The further you are from the experience, the more credible you're considered.

The Guru Economy turns borrowed wisdom into a brand asset. It positions the "thought leader" as a lone genius, no matter how many marginalized voices shaped his thinking. Harm flows downward; recognition and profit flow up.

This model disproportionately rewards people with proximity to power, those already granted legitimacy by race, class, gender, or institutional backing. It converts shared knowledge into personal capital and insulates those at the top from accountability. The result is an economy where being listened to matters more than being responsible for the impact of what you say.

<table>
<tr><td rowspan="4">journal
your
journey</td><td>Whose voices do I instinctively trust?</td></tr>
<tr><td>Where have I been tempted to hoard knowledge?</td></tr>
<tr><td>What is my intellectual lineage?</td></tr>
<tr><td>How do I want people to feel when they're with me?</td></tr>
</table>

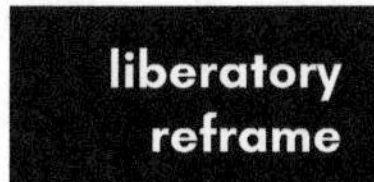

Authority Without a Pedestal

There is another way to be taken seriously. Liberatory authority rejects the idea that credibility is earned by standing above others. Instead, it's built through accountability, context, and care over time. It's about being in right relationship with self and others. This kind of authority is slower. It requires listening as much as speaking and being willing to change based on what you learn.

Liberatory authority welcomes challenges as part of its integrity. It doesn't fear being revised because it's built on responsibility, not supremacy. Being willing to change in public is part of how trust is earned and repaired over time.

In practice, this looks like moving from "I'm telling you" to "here's my addition to the conversation." One of my favorite co-conspirators, Taina Brown, helped me fully understand this distinction. She said that I don't need to be *the* voice, but I can be *one* voice in a lineage of conversation. This shift didn't make my work smaller. It made it less defensive and more honest. I didn't disappear, I became more clear about my role.

Authority isn't about self-promotion. It's about self-situating by naming your teachers, tracing your intellectual DNA, and placing your work alongside those who helped shape your thinking. Rather than diluting your credibility, the liberatory model deepens it. By shifting from leverage to lineage, your work gets richer, your voice grows sturdier, and trust multiplies. Not because you're performing certainty, but because you're practicing integrity in public.

Lineage Mapping

You didn't get here alone. Honor it by thinking through the intellectual, cultural, and relational roots of your work.

Teachers:	Ancestors:
Movements:	Conversations:
Books:	Experiences:
Communities:	Other:

The Pedestal Test

Worried you might slip into Guru Mode? Avoid it by checking these boxes:

- ☐ I'm centering the idea, not myself.
- ☐ I'm not pretending that this concept came from nowhere.
- ☐ I'm not performing a certainty that I don't actually feel.
- ☐ I'm not hoarding credit, I am freely sharing it.
- ☐ I'm not distancing myself from my community.

Audit Your Framework

Before you publish or sell anything, pause and ask these questions:

Whose work influenced this? Name the thinkers, communities, and movements that shaped the foundation you're building on. If someone's intellectual labor or lived experience is in your work, say their name.

Who's missing from this story? If your framework only reflects dominant voices, it's incomplete.

Who benefits from my version? Does your interpretation expand the circle of recognition or shrink it to spotlight you?

Who might be erased by my version? If your framework obscures the contributions of marginalized thinkers, it's time to widen the lens.

What power dynamic sits underneath this idea? Be honest about whether your framework disrupts hierarchy or reinforces it.

Authority Without Domination

Liberatory authority isn't proven by hierarchy. It's practiced through citation, accountability, and care over time. Ask yourself:

→ Where can I name my influences more clearly?

→ Who should be in conversation with this work?

→ How can I invite challenge without collapsing into defensiveness?

Authority grows when it's exercised responsibly, not when it's protected.

Micro-Liberations

Small ways break up with The Credibility Hustle and step into true leadership.

Name your lineage.
Keep a running note of the thinkers who shaped your work. Practice naming at least one of them each time you teach or write.

Retire "I created."
Most of what we teach is inherited, borrowed, or adapted. Instead of "I created," switch to "I've adapted" or "I've expanded on."

Say "I don't know" in public this month.
Credibility grows when you stop pretending you have every answer and start naming your limits with clarity.

Design with people, not for applause.
Invite feedback early. Co-create drafts or conversations with the people most impacted by the work, not just those most likely to praise it.

Cite Black women first.
Set a standard that before you reference white men you'll check whether Black women have already articulated the idea and cite them instead.

Build rooms, not audiences.
Shift one conversation, shared doc, or group effort from a broadcast to a gathering. Authority grows through proximity, not elevation.

Forget being a thought leader, become a *thought partner*. The Credibility Hustle tricks us into believing that our authority lives in isolation and originality. In reality, the most powerful work comes from shared learning.

When you tell the truth about where your work comes from, you reconnect yourself to the world that raised you. Liberatory authority isn't about proving you're real. It's about refusing to pretend you got here alone. The work isn't to rise above your people, it's to rise with them.

If you do only one thing from this chapter, do this:
Name your teachers and influences.
Credibility isn't proven by standing alone.

16.

The Power Load

Before I became a business owner, my understanding of leadership came from a long line of terrible bosses in Corporate America. There was a micromanager who second-guessed every decision I made. A boss who unhelpfully liked to say, "I don't know what I want, but I'll know it when I see it." A CEO who promised his door was always open, yet provided zero transparency with each new round of layoffs. And the worst? A new boss who told us we had to start reporting our actions down to the minute, including when we used the restroom. (I quit that job that day).

I never experienced flexibility, agency, or humanity. Each day of working for someone else felt like being a child afraid of upsetting her punitive parents. They treated mistakes as moral failures, and compliance as professionalism. I learned that safety (and career advancement) came from obedience.

When I decided to work for myself, I carried that dysfunction with me. I had no idea how to be a healthy leader to myself or the communities I built. I vacillated between being a harsh parent to myself, and being a defiant teenager who rejected those experiences by working from bed or not at all. I didn't want to recreate what I'd lived through, but I didn't yet know what could replace it.

What I did know was what leadership wasn't supposed to feel like. I didn't want control, surveillance, or fear to be the price of getting work done. But without another model, I kept defaulting to the only ones I'd seen. I tried to motivate myself with pressure. I confused discipline with punishment and accountability with self-denial. When things went well, I pushed harder. When things stalled, I assumed I was failing at leadership all over again. Without intending to, I recreated the same power dynamics and turned them inward.

There was no relief in being the boss. It was a quieter, more private version of the same pressure. Different rules, same fear. Leadership didn't change, it simply moved inside my head. This chapter is about a different way to lead.

A Tyrant at the Desk

"Leaders eat last." "If you want it done right, do it yourself." "Never let them see you sweat." Prevailing wisdom is that leadership means carrying the vision, holding the responsibility, and feeling all the pressure (this is true whether you have a team of one or 1,000). This is domination, not leadership. It teaches us that needing support is weakness, and that being irreplaceable is the highest form of value. That belief keeps power concentrated and people exhausted.

In the traditional hierarchical business model, leaders are made to believe they're indispensable and are praised for how much they can carry. Employees learn to mirror their leader's sacrifice, pace, and self-abandonment. This model benefits institutions by extracting stability, loyalty, and labor upward while isolating leaders from the support they need.

As with all oppressive systems, the cost is steepest for marginalized folks. Sociologist Tressie McMillan Cottom identified "the competence tax" as the unwritten expectation that marginalized people, especially Black women, must endlessly over-perform just to be seen as baseline competent. They're expected to do two jobs at once: the work they're paid for, and the invisible—and unpaid—labor of managing everyone else's comfort, conflict, and fragility.

This creates a vicious cycle. To be taken seriously, they over-work and over-deliver. Oppressive leadership models force marginalized people to reenact the systems that diminish and harm them. The model doesn't just harm people inside organizations. It follows them when they leave.

Solopreneurs become the overbearing boss *and* the overworked employee. It's the same toxic model, collapsed into one person. Over time, this kind of leadership gets normalized as strength, even when it's quietly burning people out. We stop asking whether it's working, and start asking who can survive it. Leadership needs to change.

<table>
<tr><td rowspan="4">journal
your
journey</td><td>What of my leadership style is mine vs. inherited?</td></tr>
<tr><td>Where does competence tax show up in my leadership?</td></tr>
<tr><td>How would leadership look if it felt safe in my body?</td></tr>
<tr><td>How can I lead without leaving myself behind?</td></tr>
</table>

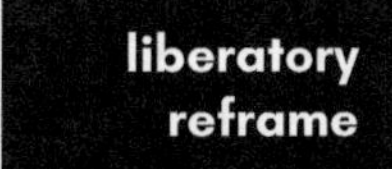

Exhausted Isn't Effective

What if leadership wasn't measured by how much you can hold, but by how well you build a culture where no one has to hold everything alone?

As Trudi Lebron writes in *The Antiracist Business Book*, liberatory leadership "uses its power to lift up, empower, include, and create opportunities." While capitalism says a leader must be the strongest and steadiest, liberation means a leader thrives inside collective responsibility.

In practice, Lebron says this shift looks like:

- Pulling back the veil on how decisions are made and inviting participation as a practice of equity.
- Communicating changes before they become crises.
- Building policies that protect people (non-negotiable starting salaries, pay transparency, clear criteria for raises not dependent on personality or proximity to power, representation goals, reimagining work schedules).
- Crafting procedures that support anti-oppressive policies.
- Tracking what actually matters (who gets promoted, who stays/goes, whose needs are overlooked, how outcomes differ across demographics).

At its core, this shift asks us to stop confusing self-sacrifice for leadership, and to recognize that sustainability is a structural question. Burnout is not a personal failure. If a system only works when someone is overextended, it's not actually working. Liberatory leadership understands that no one can lead effectively while carrying the entire weight of a system designed to endlessly extract from them. We must rebuild organizations so that everyone, regardless of position, can show up as their full selves without fear of burnout.

You're not failing at leadership when you need rest. You're practicing it.

For solopreneurs, liberatory leadership means refusing to replicate the boss/worker power dynamic inside yourself. It means setting humane timelines, planning around your actual capacity, building in rest as part of the business model, and not punishing yourself for needing support or slowness.

Liberatory leadership isn't about holding all the power or all the pressure. It trades hierarchy for wholeness by building a way of working where power circulates so that everyone, including you, gets to be human.

Power that circulates is power that transforms.

Liberatory Leadership Audit

Ask these questions to build structures where everyone, including you, thrives.
1. Where am I carrying more than my fair share?
2. What would happen if this weight were shared?
3. What decision am I making alone that could be made collaboratively?
4. Who should be in the room?
5. Whose needs or limits am I overlooking (including my own)?
6. Where is rest missing from the system?
7. Where am I hoarding information or credit? How can I redistribute it?
8. What policy, procedure, or boundary would support equity and care?

Boundaries for Better Leadership

Boundaries aren't barriers, they're the scaffolding of liberatory leadership.
- I lead at the speed of my capacity.
- I center rest as a strategic resource.
- I pause before taking on more.
- I name my limits without apology.
- I build systems that support ease.
- I communicate clearly and early.
- I make decisions from alignment, not adrenaline.
- I choose repair and transparency over perfection.
- I create space for others to contribute meaningfully.
- I distribute responsibility instead of hoarding control.

A client with a team of 60 cared deeply about building a people-first culture, so she met monthly with each team member. Sixty hours on top of running the company, leaving no time for self-care. Our work was about restoring balance; she shifted to request-based staff meetings. Despite feeling indispensable, she quickly learned that her team still felt supported even without monthly check-ins. She reclaimed massive amounts of time for big-picture work and rest. Liberation didn't mean caring less, but not treating herself like the only person who didn't deserve her care.

Micro-Liberations

Freedom begins with small, steady refusals of the old leadership paradigm.

Delegate one tiny task.
This week, hand off or automate one task you're still doing out of habit. Notice what comes up when you're no longer indispensable.

Delete before you delegate.
Before you assign something away, ask whether it even needs to exist. Make it your goal this week to remove one task entirely.

Practice transparent uncertainty.
The next time you're asked for certainty before you have it, say "I don't know yet." Let honesty replace performance.

Write your leadership rules.
How do I make decisions? What do I protect? What do I refuse? Write a statement to use as your compass when the old rules call out.

Move credit right away.
In your next email, meeting, or post, name one person whose labor is usually invisible. Say their name. Don't wait for a "bigger" moment.

Let your limits lead.
When choosing between pleasing someone or protecting your capacity, choose capacity. Watch how leadership expands instead of collapses.

When we stop replicating oppressive models, we can create a culture where all people thrive. Liberatory leadership asks us to build businesses where people matter more than performance or profits.

Whether you lead a team or just yourself, the invitation is the same. Stop trying to become the leader you were taught to admire, and start building the structures that allow everyone to thrive. When leadership becomes a site of care rather than control, something radical happens: we *all* get to breathe.

If you do only one thing from this chapter, do this:
Leadership doesn't have to hurt to be real.
Pause and notice where you've been carrying more than your share.
That awareness is part of the work.

17.

Hire Humans, Not Hustlers

For most of my career, I never had to think about hiring. I was never in a position to do the hiring, and when I was the one being hired, whiteness and privilege did most of the heavy lifting for me. I didn't recognize hiring as a system and I didn't question the process because I never needed to.

When I left Corporate America to build my own business, I brought that blind spot with me. I never learned about equitable hiring and I had no awareness of how belonging is (or isn't) built into every step of the process. I didn't yet understand that hiring isn't just about who gets chosen. It's about who was ever invited to imagine themselves inside the room.

Meeting (and eventually partnering in business with) Faith Clarke changed everything. I've watched her create belonging in every room we've shared. She co-creates intentions instead of dictating norms. She invites people to not just participate, but to co-own the experience. She tracks power and pace. She anticipates needs before they're spoken, because, as she says, belonging is "a commitment to supporting each other's needs without requiring self-advocacy." And I've seen her tell the truth about when belonging isn't yet possible.

She taught me that it's violent to invite people into a space you haven't prepared for them. That belonging isn't inevitable, and it isn't a magic trick. It's a choice, one that has to be made intentionally, through systems, rituals, and shared meaning making. Once I saw that, I couldn't unsee how often hiring does the opposite. It rewards speed over care and familiarity over imagination. It filters for people who already belong, while calling that "culture fit." And it quietly reproduces the same hierarchies it claims to be neutral about.

Most of us were never taught to see hiring this way. But once you do, it changes how you think about who gets invited in, and what responsibility comes with making that invitation. This chapter reimagines hiring as a practice of belonging, not selection, and invites us to choose differently.

The Charade of Neutrality

Oppressive management styles reward exploitation and call it "excellence," says Trudi Lebron in *The Antiracist Business Book*. Business owners are told to hire self-starters, rockstars, A-players—labels that describe endurance, not skills. They're cute ways of saying "people who will tolerate overwork without care."

The harm starts at the job posting and continues throughout the hiring process. Pay secrecy reinforces pay disparities for women and people of the global majority. Unstructured interviews lead to inconsistent evaluations and favoring first impressions. "Culture fit" reinforces conformity.

Workplaces are built on cultural norms rooted in whiteness. What's framed as neutral in hiring is simply what's normal for the dominant group. Deviation from the norm is treated as risk, but as Drs. Tina Opie and Beth Livingston say in *Shared Sisterhood*, "risk taking means that the power-dominant person was willing to put their power to work to make power dynamics more equitable."

Most hiring systems transfer risk downward. Candidates are asked to prove they can endure ambiguity, pressure, and overwork before they're offered safety, clarity, or stability. The more uncertainty a role contains, the more resilience is demanded from the person with the least power.

Capitalism flips this responsibility. Hire people who can survive harm, not people who can help prevent it. It rewards those who will absorb unclear expectations, unpaid emotional labor, and chronic overwork without complaint, while penalizing anyone who needs flexibility, clarity, or support. That's how the most marginalized candidates often lose before the interview even starts. Endurance is treated as merit, and harm is reframed as a screening tool.

Liberatory hiring requires a different lens. People aren't cogs; they're culture. Hiring isn't about finding someone who will "do it right," but about co-creating a workplace that doesn't require harm as the price of entry.

<table>
<tr><td>journal
your
journey</td><td>Do my job descriptions describe humans or machines?

Who am I unconsciously overlooking in hiring?

What would change if my hiring process centered care?

What does "belonging" mean in my business?</td></tr>
</table>

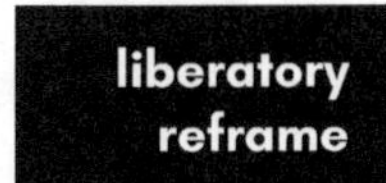

Build for Belonging

Hiring shapes culture. Liberatory leadership "uses its power to lift up, empower, include, and create opportunities," says Trudi Lebron in *The Antiracist Business Book*. People aren't resources, they're co-creators of the future you're building.

Liberatory hiring starts with transparency. Be explicit about pay, workflows, power, expectations, and growth. Let people self-select into roles with full information. It also requires designing roles for humans, not machines. Right-size responsibilities. Remove the extraction buried in "fast-paced environment," "flexible," or "team player." Name the actual skills and support someone will receive. Create job descriptions that reflect reality, not fantasy.

This kind of transparency can feel risky inside of systems that reward control. We've been taught that withholding information protects leverage, when it's actually protecting inequity. Liberatory hiring asks us to trust people with the truth, even when it complicates the process.

In a liberatory process, the employer (not the candidate) absorbs uncertainty. The goal is not to see who can tolerate the most ambiguity, but to create enough clarity that people don't have to gamble with their dignity to participate.

This approach means interrupting bias:

- Use structured interviews so gut feeling isn't shorthand for sameness.
- Replace "culture fit" with "culture contribution," a principle Dr. Tina Opie champions in *Shared Sisterhood*.
- Slow down so urgency doesn't override equity.

Prioritize co-creation over compliance. Treat candidates as collaborators-in-waiting, not risks to be managed. Invite candidates to ask questions, offer ideas, and imagine the role with you. Share your decision-making process. Be honest about pivots and possibilities.

Finally, liberatory hiring is about belonging. Not performative diversity. Belonging means people can bring their full selves into work without fear of punishment, retaliation, or invisibility. A simple litmus test is asking, will this hire make our work more humane, equitable, and spacious? If the answer is no, the process needs slowing down, redesigning, or rethinking entirely.

Liberatory hiring is not about finding the "best person." It's about building the conditions where everyone you hire becomes better because the culture allows them to be human.

Unpacking Belonging and Hiring

*with **Faith Clarke** of Work Ecosystems for Humans, who helps leaders cultivate people-first work cultures.*

Becky Mollenkamp: You invite people "on mission," vs. just hiring help. What do you mean by that?

Faith Clarke: A lot of us hire because we're desperate: I need this off my plate. That's different than inviting someone into a mission you're building together. That means asking: 'What do you want in your life? What do you care about?' Then finding the intersection between their goals and yours. If they're there to do a task for $20 an hour, that's transactional. With a shared *why*, it becomes relational. We're co-creating, not just trading time for money.

Becky: How do we decolonize hiring?

Faith: Colonized work treats people as expenses and the business as the asset. Decolonizing flips that so people are the asset and their nourishment is core. In hiring, it looks like co-creating terms of work vs. dictating them, designing roles that can evolve, and questioning each place people must ask permission for time or resources. When people have to ask permission, like for time off to tend to children or a medical need, that's a sign of hierarchy and extraction.

Becky: How do we make compensation less extractive?

Faith: Money doesn't land the same in every life. One person may need tuition or therapy, while someone else might need childcare support. Liberatory hiring asks what each person needs to be whole enough to do the work. That doesn't mean becoming their savior. It means you listen deeply and, where you can, shape compensation and benefits in ways that nourish humans, not just roles.

Becky: For solo business owners, how do we know when to hire at all?

Faith: If you're hiring because you're in panic, 'I just need a VA right now,' you'll almost always recreate the same extractive patterns you left in corporate. Slow down to ask: What am I really building? What kind of relationship do I want with the people who work with me? Am I willing to invite them into the mission, not just tasks? If you're unwilling to do that, you may not be ready to hire.

Micro-Liberations

Shift how you hire and build with people you bring into your work.

Name the human before the role.
Before reviewing applicants, define 3 to 5 human qualities that matter for this work. Use these as your anchor when decisions get fuzzy.

Write humane job descriptions.
Delete vague phrases like fast-paced, wear many hats, or rockstar and replace them with specific tasks and a realistic weekly workload.

Name your power.
At the start of interviews, name what you control (pay, scope, timeline) and commit to using that power to create clarity.

Ask questions that reveal fit, not endurance.
Swap "How do you handle pressure?" for "What kind of support helps you do your best work?" Listen for needs, not toughness.

Build a shared rubric.
Choose 4 to 6 criteria in advance and score each candidate the same way. Consistency reduces bias more than gut instinct ever will.

Co-create the role.
Ask the candidate: "What would make this role sustainable for you?" Begin collaboration before the offer is signed.

Every hiring choice either recreates the systems that harmed you, or moves you closer to the culture you're trying to build. You don't need workers who can hustle harder; you need people who can build belonging with you.

Liberatory hiring is slow, intentional, and relational. It recognizes that great teams are made of humans who care and share power. The invitation is to hire in a way that honors the belief that work should never demand humanity as the price of admission.

If you do only one thing from this chapter, do this:
Design one role or process around human capacity instead of endurance.

Interlude

After I Couldn't Unsee It

Everything didn't change all at once. Meaningful change rarely does. But the phone call in the early morning hours of July 4, 2010 cracked something open that would never fully close. My brother died of a heroin overdose at 30 years old. That loss didn't liberate me, but it shattered the story I'd been living inside. The one that told me "good enough" was the best I could hope for, and that survival was the same thing as safety.

In the years that followed, almost everything I had built collapsed. My marriage ended. I was depressed. The Great Recession decimated my freelance business. I went from earning over $100,000 in 2009 to less than $13,000 the following year. I lost the house I had poured my sense of success into. I lost friendships that were tied more tightly to the life I was leaving than the person I actually was, and I grieved them longer than I expected.

For a long stretch of time, I tried to outrun my grief the only way I knew how. I worked late nights, stayed busy, numbed myself, and pretended avoidance was the same thing as healing. It didn't work.

What I was forced to confront, slowly and painfully, was that awareness alone doesn't save you. Knowing the system is broken doesn't protect you from its consequences. And unlearning doesn't arrive as clarity, it begins as disorientation, loss, and a deep reckoning with what you can no longer carry.

Just before my 38th birthday, I made a decision that felt both humbling and necessary. I moved back into my mom's home. It was a privilege to have that option, and it came with its own grief. I was surviving on very little income, letting go of the identity I had built through achievement, and giving myself time to grieve my brother's death. For the first time in my adult life, I wasn't performing resilience. I allowed myself to sit with uncertainty.

I didn't use that time to "fix" myself. Instead, I gained a new relationship with myself. For the first time, my sense of worth wasn't dependent on output, praise, or performance. I began to gain a deep, embodied understanding that the emptiness I'd spent decades trying to outrun wasn't a personal failure. It was the predictable outcome of living inside a system that taught me to confuse worth with productivity, safety with money, and belonging with performance.

That realization didn't hand me a blueprint for what came next, but it gave me permission. I stopped trying to build a life that looked successful on paper, yet required constant self-betrayal to maintain. I became less focused on proving I was enough, and more focused on choosing work, relationships, and rhythms that didn't require me to disappear. I didn't know exactly what I was building, but I knew what I was no longer sacrificing to get there.

My re-education didn't happen through one framework or philosophy. It happened through listening and lineage. Through Black women who know what it means to build belonging in places not designed for them, like bell hooks, Audre Lorde, adrienne maree brown, and Mia Birdsong. Through thinkers and scholars who asked better questions about running a business that reflect feminist values, like Jennifer Armbrust's *Proposals for the Feminine Economy*, CV Harquail's *Feminism: A Key Idea in Business*, and Kelly Diels' essays and emails. Through teachings that insisted pace, consent, and interdependence were not weaknesses, but strengths.

What this wise women's council taught me is that you can't skip the part where everything is unclear. The space between collapse and creation is uncomfortable and it can be lonely, but it's also fertile. It's where the real stuff lives. It's where honesty can show up because you've stopped waiting to have it all figured out before you let yourself begin. As it turns out, that's exactly the right condition for something true to grow.

By my 40th birthday, nothing about my life looked the way it had five years earlier. I was in a healthy, steady relationship. I was letting go of professional writing and stepping into coaching. I was trying to have a baby. None of it felt linear or certain, but it felt honest in a way my earlier successes never had.

Today, I'm married to that partner, and we're raising the most amazing child together. I have work that feels deeply fulfilling, not because it's impressive on paper, but because it's aligned with how I want to live. I work with founders who share the same quiet desire: to work in ways that feel human.

That work looks less like optimization and more like relationship. Less like fixing and more like listening. We explore self-compassion, power dynamics, consent, and capacity not as abstract ideas, but as daily practices that shape how people lead, decide, and care for themselves and others.

Along the way, I began building in community instead of in isolation. I co-run Feminist Founders with Faith Clarke and Messy Liberation Coaches Circle with Taina Brown. Expertise circulates and leadership is shared. The work became more joyful, rigorous, and sustainable the moment it stopped being a solo act. Likewise, I founded Feminist Podcasters Collective as a community where all voices are heard and given weight in decisions.

It took me years to understand that what I had once labeled as personal failure was actually predictable conditioning. I wasn't broken, but I'd been taught to confuse worth with productivity, safety with money, and belonging with performance. The system rewarded me when I complied and punished me when I didn't. I internalized those rules long before I ever ran a business.

I no longer try to fill my cup by pleasing others or playing a part. I fill it by choosing work and relationships that don't require self-erasure. By building slower, telling the truth, and letting life be textured instead of optimized.

This book exists because I stopped asking, "What's wrong with me?" and started asking, "What kind of system makes so many of us feel this way?" Once you ask that question honestly, the future shifts from a destination you have to earn into something you can practice, together.

Everything that follows turns toward that future. Not as a promise or a prescription, but as an invitation to imagine what becomes possible when we stop trying to survive systems that were never built for our flourishing, and begin practicing something else (something better) instead.

Section 4

The Future We Can Choose

Liberation is a practice, not something you arrive at all at once. Liberation doesn't mean pretending the cage never existed. It means noticing when the door is open, and trusting yourself enough to decide whether and how to move. After naming how we were shaped, exposing the lies we were sold, and dismantling extractive business myths, this final section turns toward possibility.

What does it look like to build a business that feels like home instead of a performance? What changes when you honor your capacity, body, joy, and relationships instead of productivity theater and endurance as virtue?

Much of what this section names is already happening in mutual aid networks, collectives, and care-rooted practices that rarely get labeled as successful. Here, we choose a different future on purpose. You'll reconnect with your True North, practice boundaries as a strategy, reclaim pleasure as a source of power, and build collaborative structures that resist isolation. We'll explore accountability as repair (not punishment), activism as a daily practice (not a branding move), and legacy as something shaped through care (not empire).

This section doesn't ask you to become someone new. It asks you to remember what you already know about care, capacity, and belonging so you can build from there.

18.

Start with Values

There were two days that forced me to get honest about what really mattered to me. The first was July 10, 2010 when my brother died of an overdose (at the same time my first marriage was ending). Grief makes you ask, "what do I really want from life?" and I didn't have an answer. I'd been moving through life on autopilot, as a good girl. I'd never named my values or noticed how far I'd drifted from them.

Once autopilot broke, I couldn't put it back together. The life I'd been living no longer felt survivable, let alone meaningful.

The second was Aug. 9, 2014 when a police officer gunned down Michael Brown less than a mile from my front door. My eyes finally opened to the systems I benefit from, and to my complicity in replicating them, despite running phone banks for Bill Clinton's second presidential run, and spending countless weekends knocking on doors for Barack Obama's first.

Following each of these pivotal days, I got quiet, asked myself hard questions, and journaled until answers revealed themselves. In 2010, I realized that money, stability, and an important job aren't worth hiding away parts of myself. *Authenticity* and *courage* are my core values. In 2014, I realized that voting "blue no matter who" isn't the same as "none of us is free until we're all free," and that I care far more about the latter. *Liberation* and *community* are also my core values.

More than words on a website, values are a compass. They point you back to your True North when you've forgotten yourself or when everything feels impossible. We still get pulled back into capitalist conditioning sometimes; we're swimming in the same waters, after all. But when values are named, we can feel misalignment sooner (it shows up as shoulds, resentment, or tension), trace it back to what's being betrayed, and course-correct faster.

Values don't necessarily make business or life easier. But they do make them truer, and something you can live inside without losing yourself.

141

The Alignment Illusion

Many companies treat values as little more than a list of words that look good on a website. When this happens, they name them once rather than practicing them daily. They say community, but maintain extractive marketing practices. They say equity, but don't ask who's missing from the room. They say rest, but reward burnout. In a culture where white-supremacist capitalist patriarchy defines what is considered professional, values become a way to look good while doing harm.

Our oppressive culture trains us to separate intention from impact. Values get treated as private beliefs, while business habits follow the logic of efficiency, urgency, and self-protection. As adrienne maree brown reminds us in *Emergent Strategy* "what we practice at the small scale sets the patterns for the whole system." Business leaders drift out of alignment because dominant culture rewards them for abandoning what matters most, and punishes those who stay true to their human-first values.

This is how values become decorative instead of directive. They show up on websites and in brand language, but aren't a meaningful part of budgets or policies. Over time, people inside the business learn that alignment is optional, but performance is required. Most businesses rely on values that cost nothing.

As Mona Eltahawy reminds us in *The Seven Necessary Sins for Women and Girls*, a real commitment to dismantling systems of oppression requires a conscious refusal to comply with, comfort, or be nice to those systems. "Racism and bigotry are not polite, and I refuse to be polite in my fight against them."

Dr. Barbara J. Love teaches that liberatory consciousness is a practice built through ongoing awareness, analysis, action, and accountability. In that model, values are daily commitments. They shape how you make decisions, spend money, and relate to your community. Values are not what you say you care about. They're what you resource, repeat, protect, and practice.

<table>
<tr><td rowspan="4">journal
your
journey</td><td>Which of my values do I not practice consistently?</td></tr>
<tr><td>Which values feel risky to live out loud?</td></tr>
<tr><td>Who pays the price when my values aren't practiced?</td></tr>
<tr><td>What micro-habits would help me live into my values?</td></tr>
</table>

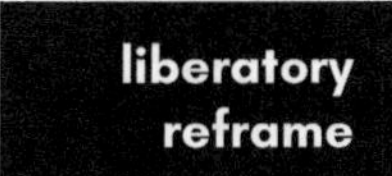

Practice Not Perfection

Running a liberatory business inside an oppressive system necessitates a constant negotiation between values and survival. Some days you can choose the values path. Other days you must take the rent-is-due path.

That doesn't make you a fraud, it makes you human. Liberation isn't about perfection or performance, so we return to Dr. Barbara J. Love's Liberatory Consciousness model as a roadmap:

1. Awareness: Notice when survival is steering the wheel instead of values. "I'm choosing speed over equity," or "I'm saying yes because I can't afford to lose the income." Name it without judgement.

2. Analysis: Name the forces shaping your choice. Whose comfort or safety are you prioritizing? What identities or privileges make this risky or doable? Distinguish between conditioning (urgency, people-pleasing, scarcity) and systemic constraints (racism, ableism, financial disparity).

3. Action: Choose the most values-aligned option you can. Not the perfect choice, but the possible one. Maybe you can't turn down a misaligned client, but you can set clearer boundaries. Maybe you can't overhaul your systems, but you can remove the most extractive tactic.

4. Accountability: Tell the truth about why you made the choice, acknowledge the impact, and adjust your systems so the next choice is easier.

Privilege changes the cost of values-aligned choices. Part of this work is knowing which risks you can take, and which you should not expect others to absorb. Liberation doesn't demand that we all make the same choices, but that we get honest about uneven consequences.

The work is to know which choices are constrained by the system, and which are shaped by conditioning, and to refuse shame either way.

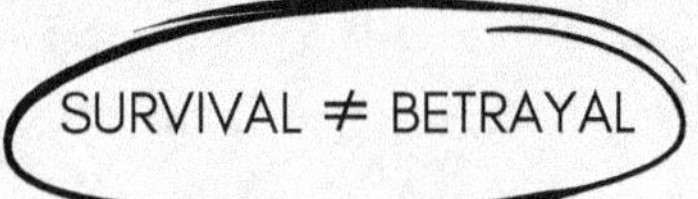

Choosing survival does not cancel your values. Paying your bills, protecting your capacity, or avoiding harm is not "selling out." It's responding to the conditions you're in.

Determining Your Values

Here's a guide to help you identify the core commitments that shape your decisions, leadership, community, and culture.

Start with Lived Experience

Reflect on the moments in your life when things felt aligned, and identify what value was being honored in those moments.

Make a Messy, Expansive List

Write down every value word that is revealed during the reflection process. Add any others that feel aspirational or are what you desire for work and life. Don't edit yet. Let it be indulgent.

Group and Cluster Words

Look for themes and relationships. What belongs together? Which words feel like expressions of something larger? This helps you uncover the deeper root values beneath the surface-level ones.

Cut Ruthlessly

Group like words to identify the one that feels most accurate. Delete any that don't really affect how you want to lead or live, or those that are personality traits rather than values.

Reduce to 3(ish) Values

Nearly every conviction you hold can be mapped back to a few foundational values. Those are what matter. More becomes noise.

Define Behaviors for Each Value

Finish the sentence: "Our business practices this value when we…" or "I practice this value when I…" to turn words into actionable value statements.

If this process feels uncomfortable, that's a sign you're doing it honestly. When you finish, though, you'll have values that aren't about branding, aesthetics, or optics. You'll have values that reorient your leadership, systems, and business toward liberation, one daily practice at a time.

Micro-Liberations

Small choices made on busy days can shift values from theory into practice.

Translate values into behaviors.
Pick one value and write three actions that prove it's real (how you price, schedule, or communicate). If it can't be seen, it's not guiding you yet.

Audit your systems.
Choose one system this week (marketing, onboarding, scheduling), name where it contradicts your values, and devise a plan to create alignment.

Practice an act of refusal.
Strengthen your 'no' muscle by rejecting a values-violating request, whether that's an unrealistic timeline or a scope-busting add-on.

Name your non-negotiables.
Tell clients, collaborators, or your audience one boundary you won't cross. Clarity builds trust faster than accommodation.

Design a weekly values ritual.
Set a recurring 15-minute check-in to ask: "Where did I act in alignment this week? Where did I drift?" Course-correction is the practice.

Resource one value.
Allocate money or time to a value you care about (accessibility, rest, pay equity). What you resource becomes real.

Values name what matters, and help you guide decisions, shape systems, and provide a way back to yourself when you drift. They expose where you're abandoning yourself to meet expectations you never agreed to. They reveal where your business is aligned with liberation, and where it's operating on inherited scripts that don't serve you or your community.

Business is crafted through thousands of small choices. Values are a compass to your True North, and putting them into practice is the path to get there.

19.

Boundaries are Strategy

I have Generalized Anxiety Disorder and ADHD, and I'm an INJF and Enneagram 6. That adds up to me being full of worry, highly sensitive, and deeply introverted. I know how to wear a calm, collected and confident mask, but it's heavy so wearing it for too long is exhausting. That mask has always been part of my survival strategy, in life and work. And like most coping mechanisms praised by dominant culture, it worked ... until it didn't.

The mask broke in the fall of 2023 when I launched Feminist Founders podcast. After months of intense creation, I moved into a hectic promotion schedule, hosting a live launch party for 50+ people, doing a dozen live social media chats, and sharing on social media multiple times a day. All while also parenting and running the paying parts of my business.

My typical methods for calming my nervous system (no caffeine, walks, deep breathing) didn't work. I experienced TMJ, back pain, headaches, GI issues, sleeping difficulties, lightheadedness, and heart palpitations. My body quit because I ignored every earlier signal asking me to slow down. I asked my husband to pick our son up from school so I could take a warm shower. It wasn't enough. I lay down, closed my eyes, placed my hands over my heart, and reassured myself that I was safe. During that anxiety attack, I had to confront a hard truth: I needed to set better boundaries. I asked my husband to take on all household and parenting tasks that evening so that I could lie there without guilt. He thanked me for asking for help.

The next day, I made an appointment with my doctor, who prescribed anti-depressant medication. I asked my business besties for help with an offer, which brought in needed income. And I released a few tasks to reduce overwhelm.

Our oppressive culture affirms the Superwoman sacrifice as righteous. That makes it difficult for us to ask for help or set boundaries without shame. Liberation teaches that boundaries aren't selfish, but a practice of worthiness.

Demanding Obedience

Boundaries aren't distributed equitably. If a cishet, able-bodied white man says no, he's considered decisive and someone who knows his worth. Someone else asserting the same boundary, however, is perceived very differently:

- If you're Black, you're angry or unprofessional.
- If you're a woman, you're difficult.
- If you're neurodiverse, you're inflexible.
- If you're disabled or chronically ill, you're unreliable.
- If you're queer or trans, you're dramatic.

The same behavior is judged not by its impact, but by who is daring to assert it.

Oppressive systems depend on people with marginalized identities fearing those consequences. If you're scared to be misunderstood or to disappoint, then you'll keep saying yes long after your body starts screaming no. And if you're always giving, accommodating, and performing emotional labor, you'll have no energy left to challenge the conditions creating the harm.

The expectation that you should always say yes is the legacy of systems that treated certain humans as property or tools (enslaved people, domestic workers, immigrants, disabled people, women). Boundaries are survival infrastructure. They're how we protect our bodies, time, energy, and dignity. They help us stay alive in systems that treat us like resources instead of people. And they allow us to reclaim agency in contexts designed to strip it away.

Systems built on domination rely on blurred boundaries. If you start saying no, you disrupt the flow of unpaid labor that keeps these systems functioning. When someone punishes you for asserting a limit, what they're really saying is: "My comfort matters more than your capacity."

You were never meant to be endlessly available. Boundaries don't make you selfish. They make you free.

<table>
<tr><td rowspan="4">journal
your
journey</td><td>What boundary have I been taught is "too much"?</td></tr>
<tr><td>What might change if I had boundaries that serve me?</td></tr>
<tr><td>What boundaries am I craving?</td></tr>
<tr><td>What do I need to feel safe to share my boundaries?</td></tr>
</table>

Love Not Limitations

We're taught that boundaries push people away, that saying "no" is selfish, that protecting ourselves is somehow a betrayal of community. That's oppression talking. Capitalism needs people who are endlessly available, emotionally flexible, and willing to quietly absorb harm. It calls that generosity. It rewards those who overextend and shames those who stop agreeing to their own depletion.

Boundaries aren't punitive, they're relationship-protecting tools. "Boundaries require us to rework and restructure our relationships for the sake of connection, for deep mutuality," Prentis Hemphill wrote in *What it Takes to Heal.* They interrupt the assumption that access is automatic and care is infinite. They force honesty about capacity, power, and consent.

You can't practice mutuality if you're depleted, offer care if you're collapsing, or build collective liberation by abandoning yourself. Boundaries teach people how to be in relationship with the *real* you, not a stressed-out, burned-out version that capitalism tries to mold you into. Without boundaries, connection becomes performance, and care becomes coercion.

Further, boundaries are declarations of worthiness. They say, "My body, time, energy, and humanity belong to me." In a culture that endlessly extracts, especially from the most marginalized, that is revolutionary. Every time you assert a boundary that protects your right to rest, to space, to change your mind, to your own pace, or to your own needs, you weaken the oppressor's story that only certain people get to be human without consequences.

This matters because who is "allowed" boundaries is not evenly distributed. Women, caregivers, disabled folks, and people of the global majority are disproportionately expected to be flexible, accommodating, and endlessly patient, even at great personal cost. When they set limits, they're labeled difficult, ungrateful, or unprofessional. Boundaries disrupt that extraction by making exploitation visible and harder to justify.

Liberation asks us to build lives and businesses where everyone's needs matter, including our own. Boundaries are the architecture of that world. They aren't about keeping people out. They're about helping you stay whole enough to let the right people in and stay in relationship without disappearing.

Boundaries don't end connection; they make it sustainable.

Boundary Blueprint

1. SET: Clarify the boundary you need.
Most boundaries start with you. Before you say anything to another person, identify what you need to feel safe, grounded, and whole, and what resources (rest, time, support, space) will help you achieve it. If you're unsure what boundary you need, start with your body. Where do you feel tension, resentment, or dread? Those sensations are often your first boundary signals. Types of boundaries to consider:

→ *Internal:* Relationship with yourself (self-care, time management, etc.)

→ *Emotional:* Giving/receiving advice, blame, judgment, guilt, etc.

→ *Mental:* Discussing thoughts, values, and opinions.

→ *Physical:* Personal space, privacy, and body.

→ *Sexual:* What, where, when, and with whom you allow sexual activity.

→ *Material:* Lending, giving, and receiving of money and things.

2. SHARE: Communicate the boundary clearly and without apology.
If the boundary involves another person, tell them confidently. Be forceful and assertive, while also being respectful (no yelling or hurling insults). Clarity and kindness are more effective than over-explanation and defensiveness. Your boundary is not a debate, and it doesn't need to make sense to anyone else. But stay open to updating it as you learn more about your needs or circumstances.

3. SUSTAIN: Follow through if the boundary is crossed.
Boundaries aren't about controlling another person's behavior. You can only decide how you'll respond if they don't respect your wishes.

→ A preference: *"I'd like this."*

→ A boundary: *"I need this."*

→ A punishment: *"You must do this."*

Know in advance what you'll do (log off, change the topic, decline future invitations, step away from the relationship). Boundaries only work if you honor the commitment, not because the other person magically behaves better.

If you feel guilt or shame about enforcing a boundary, reframe it:

→ I'm being difficult *becomes* I'm being clear.

→ I owe them an explanation *becomes* I owe them honesty.

→ I should be able to handle more *becomes* Capacity is not a moral issue.

→ They'll be upset *becomes* Their feelings aren't my instructions.

Boundary Scripts

"I need ______. If ______ happens, I will ______."

"I don't work outside my business hours. If you message me after 5pm, I'll respond the next business day."

"I need respect. If you continue to speak to me this way, I'll end this chat."

"I don't do unpaid labor. If you'd like to 'pick my brain,' here is my rate."

"I don't participate in events that require me to perform urgency or manipulation. If that's part of the marketing plan, I'll pass."

"I'm stepping out for the rest of the day for my mental health. If you need me, I'll be available to talk tomorrow."

"Feedback is welcome. If the tone becomes disrespectful, however, I will end the conversation."

"Payment is due before work begins. If the invoice isn't paid by the due date, the timeline will need to be extended."

"If payments are late more than once, I will pause work until we re-establish a sustainable plan."

"My pronouns aren't optional. If they're repeatedly ignored, we can't continue working together."

"I don't accept voice notes longer than 2 minutes. If you need more space, please send an email instead."

"I don't attend meetings without an agenda. If there isn't one, let's reschedule once clarity is in place."

"Please don't refer clients to me without checking my capacity first. If it continues, I'll remove myself from your referral list."

"My accommodations aren't optional. If they can't be met, I won't attend."

"I don't allow myself to be the 'only one' in harmful rooms. If there's no plan for safety, inclusion, or accountability, I won't enter."

Boundaries aren't...	Boundaries are...
Mean, rude, hurtful.	Useful in attracting people who respect you and repelling those who don't.
Limiting.	Meant to protect your joy by aligning your relationships and experiences with your values.
Absolute.	Based on an individual's perspective, values, and needs. They vary from person to person.
Set in stone.	Allowed to change. They will necessarily evolve as you do.

Signs a Boundary is Needed

✓ Saying yes when you really want to say no (or vice versa).
✓ Doing something only to please someone else or out of fear of rejection.
✓ Feeling annoyed, angry, resentful, or guilty about a person or situation.
✓ Feeling like a victim of a person or situation.
✓ Struggling to make a decision.
✓ Getting embroiled in someone else's drama.
✓ Feeling out of alignment with your core values.

The Boundary Spectrum

The goal is not perfect boundaries, but responsive ones.

RIGID	← HEALTHY →	POROUS
Trusts no one, even those closest to them.	Takes time to build trust.	Overly trusting, even of strangers.
Always immediately says 'no' and feels cut off.	Says 'no' when it feels self-honoring to do so.	Rarely says 'no' and grows resentful.
Isolates to avoid conflict and rejection.	Remains true to self, regardless of consequences.	Easily concedes to avoid conflict.
Ignores everyone's opinions.	Balances others' input with internal knowing.	Dependent on the opinions of others.

Micro-Liberations

Boundaries require small, honest choices that honor your capacity in real time.

Practice one truthful sentence.
When a full no feels scary, try "I don't have capacity for that," or "I need more time." Truth builds self-trust faster than explanations.

Stop explaining, start stating.
Skip the backstory. "I'm not available for that" is complete. Repeating yourself is optional; defending yourself is not.

Pause before promising.
Before you say yes, check in with your body. Is it tight or open? Is there dread or ease? Urgency or clarity? Let sensation guide the decision.

Create containers, not walls.
Offer structure instead of overgiving: "I can do 10 minutes," "Email works best," "I'll reply tomorrow."

Use repair instead of perfection.
You'll set a boundary imperfectly, over-explain it, or walk it back. "I want to restate that more clearly" prioritizes relationships, not shame.

Honor your body's no.
When your jaw tightens, your stomach drops, or your shoulders rise, treat it as data. Capacity is not a character flaw.

The world has taught many of us to treat our needs like inconveniences and our limits like personal failures. That's by design. If you're exhausted, you won't resist. Boundaries break that cycle.

Every time you honor a limit, you practice believing that your humanity is non-negotiable. Every time you say no to something that depletes you, you say yes to something that sustains you. Every time you tell the truth about what you can hold, you make space for relationships built on mutuality.

20.

Pleasure is Power

Four times a year, I check into a hotel a few miles from my house for a weekend. Two nights alone. No laundry. No driving a kid to soccer practice. No making meals. No one needing anything from me. Just me, myself, and a thermostat cranked down to "ice cube" for perimenopause relief.

I started doing these retreats after my husband, recognizing my overwhelm, gifted me with a one-night hotel stay for my third Mother's Day. I cried being away from my kiddo, but I also had a decadent time drinking wine and watching Netflix in bed. That night, I realized that I'd lost touch with myself in the busyness of parenting, incrementally, in the way that happens when everyone else's needs become the loudest thing in the room.

So I committed to repeating the solo hotel time on a regular basis. Quickly I discovered that two nights was better, giving me enough time to pamper myself, catch up on rest, and also do some big-picture dreaming for my business (the stuff that never gets done in the day-to-day chaos of work).

It didn't take long for my solo retreats to become a non-negotiable. They help me stay connected to Becky ... the person I am beyond Mom, Wife, Daughter, Friend, Coach, and the myriad other titles I hold. And they allow time for rest and solitude, which I don't give myself often enough. Without this time, my work shrinks, my patience frays, and my leadership weakens. It's been seven years since that first solo hotel stay, so I've now had more than 20 of these glorious weekends. Every time I share about them on social media or in conversation, other women and business owners say, "I need that!" That tells me a lot about how many of us are running on empty and calling it fine.

Rest isn't a luxury. Pleasure isn't indulgence. Restoration isn't negotiable. We're allowed to feel good, to tend to ourselves, to slow down even when the world demands speed. These practices aren't treats. They're what make the rest of our lives and our work possible.

Exhaustion Is Compliance

Rest and pleasure have always been rationed commodities, reserved only for those whom white-supremacist capitalist patriarchy deems worthy. This rationing is a core feature of how domination maintains itself. A rested body has more capacity to resist, remember, and imagine possibilities.

Oppressors denied enslaved people rest as a matter of law. They excluded domestic and agricultural laborers from early labor protection laws, cementing rest inequity into federal policy. Even now, studies show that sleep and rest disparities correlate with race and class. "A legacy of exhaustion resides somewhere in all of us, but specifically resides in the bodies of those who have melanated skin," writes Tricia Hersey in *Rest is Resistance.*

Women were also pushed into unpaid labor (parenting and household work) through both policy and expectation. Even after entering the workforce, women performed a "second shift" long before Arlie Hochschild gave it a name, doing an average of two extra hours of unpaid work a day compared to men. As always, Black, immigrant, and low-income women carry the heaviest load.

Disabled and chronically ill people have been structurally denied rest through both economic coercion and outright punishment. The disability benefits system ties survival to productivity tests, forcing people to prove their exhaustion again and again. Many disabled folks work while sick because opting out means losing income, healthcare, or legal status.

Rest and pleasure have become status symbols. Those with the greatest means can attend yoga retreats, have spa days, or take afternoon naps. The people most harmed by oppression are the least able to access the very things that would allow them to repair from it. "One day I hope we can all deprogram from the lie that rest, silence, and pausing is a luxury and privilege. It is not! The systems manipulated you to believe it is true," Hersey says.

<table>
<tr><td rowspan="4">journal
your
journey</td><td>Who and what suffers when I deny myself ease?</td></tr>
<tr><td>Where does rest feel dangerous or irresponsible to me?</td></tr>
<tr><td>What have I been waiting to "earn"?</td></tr>
<tr><td>How can I treat my body as collaborator vs. obstacle?</td></tr>
</table>

Aliveness Is Rebellion

Systems of oppression aren't afraid of our exhaustion, but of our aliveness. "Loving ourselves and each other deepens our disruption of the dominant systems," writes Tricia Hersey in *Rest is Resistance*. "They want us unwell, fearful, exhausted, and without deep self-love because you are easier to manipulate when you are distracted by what is not real or true."

Rest is not equally radical for everyone. White women with relative safety, flexibility, and financial cushion have co-opted Hersey's manifesto to frame rest as a personal rebellion, removed from the systems that make rest accessible to some and impossible for others. When rest is severed from power, it's flattened into another girlboss aesthetic rather than a political demand.

Rest without redistribution becomes self-soothing, not transformation. It offers relief without repair, and comfort without consequence. It leaves intact the systems that decide who gets to slow down and who must keep running.

Capitalism is disrupted not just when some people rest, but when those with privilege use their access to reduce harm for others. The more power you hold, the less liberation is about protecting your own rest and the more it's about changing the conditions that deny rest to those with less privilege. That means rethinking pace, expectations, boundaries, hiring practices, deadlines, and what we silently reward or normalize in our businesses and communities.

Rest and pleasure still matter deeply. They interrupt capitalism's demand that worth be measured in output. "You were not just born to center your entire existence on work and labor," Hersey reminds us. "You were born to heal, to grow, to dream, and to connect." Pleasure is information, says adrienne maree brown. What feels good can guide us toward what is sustainable and life-giving.

But liberation asks more than personal permission to pause. It asks us to reject the lie that exhaustion is inevitable and sacrifice is noble. As Hersey writes, "Release the shame you feel when resting. It does not belong to you." Shame is just another tool of control.

"We must believe we are worthy of rest," Hersey says. "We don't have to earn it. It is our birthright." Liberation isn't everyone resting the same way, but staying awake to the unequal distribution of time, safety, and choice. Making rest accessible to all requires more than individual healing. It requires those with power to help build conditions where rest isn't reserved for them.

Unpacking Rest as Liberation

*with **Jordan Maney,** a coach who helps bleeding hearts rest for recovery, release, and reclamation.*

Becky Mollenkamp: Why do we feel like rest is selfish?

Jordan Maney: Most of us were raised with a work ethic, but not a rest ethic. And if you talk to people from marginalized backgrounds, rest wasn't modeled as a right. It was something only certain people were allowed to have. We've inherited generations of belief that rest is laziness or sin. Even when we want to rest, our body says: 'How dare you?'

Becky: What do you mean by 'rest is liberation'?

Jordan: Historically, a lot of us weren't allowed to say no, so for people with marginalized identities, having agency over your body, time, and energy is radical. Rest is how we remember we're human, not tools for others' comfort.

Becky: How is what you talk about different than girlboss self-care?

Jordan: Whatever you think rest is, throw it out. Rest isn't just bubble baths. Rest is nourishment. It's the energy, attention, and time you give to yourself. It's what allows you to keep going without abandoning yourself.

Becky: Why do people feel guilty or afraid of pleasure?

Jordan: We've been taught pleasure is dirty, indulgent, or dangerous. That's especially true for people with marginalized identities and anyone raised in purity culture. Pleasure is treated like a moral failing. But pleasure is deeply restorative. It's part of how we return to ourselves. I always say that rest and pleasure don't make you soft. They make you sustainable.

Becky: You and I talk a lot about joy as resistance. What does that mean?

Jordan: Joy is light, and the perfect place for it to show up is in the dark. We're living through so much grief, instability, and collective pain, but joy runs parallel to all of it. You don't wait for the light at the end of the tunnel. You become the light. Making room for moments of delight, connection, and laughter is how we survive the world without hardening.

Micro-Liberations

Try these small acts of rest and pleasure and give yourself the gift of resistance.

Stop glamorizing exhaustion.
Once this week, notice when you say "I'm busy" or joke about exhaustion. Replace it with: "I'm tired and working on changing that."

Redefine in real time.
When you catch yourself thinking "I'm being lazy," consciously swap in "I'm resting" or "I'm recovering." Language rewires shame.

Treat rest as non-negotiable.
Put at least 30 minutes of rest on your calendar this week. Treat it like a client meeting—no rescheduling unless you'd cancel a paid call.

Reclaim the erotic.
Pick one daily pleasure that produces nothing—a hot shower, music with your eyes closed, stretching, sex, sunlight. No multitasking allowed.

Ask your body, not your to-do list.
Once per day, ask "What do I need right now?" Then meet that need at the smallest possible scale (one breath, one stretch, one glass of water).

Practice being unavailable.
Choose a specific hour this week where you don't reply, scroll, post, or caretake. Put your phone away. Let nothing happen on purpose.

Inside a system that demands obedience, tiredness is a moral failure and ease is earned. Capitalism makes you believe that you should feel grateful for scraps, ashamed of needing rest, and suspicious of your own pleasure.

Rest and pleasure help you return to the you that's never been colonized, commodified, or exhausted beyond repair. They're how you remember that you aren't a machine built for extraction. A business built without pleasure eventually cannibalizes the people inside it, including you.

If you do only one thing from this chapter, do this:
Choose one small pleasure this week and take it without apology.
Pay attention to what shifts when you don't justify it.

21.

Curiosity and Creativity

I grew up believing I wasn't creative. That felt like the domain of my younger brother, a poet. His mind worked sideways and beautifully, and the world punished him for it. Teachers labeled him difficult and disruptive. He was repeatedly disciplined, and eventually expelled from school.

Watching that happen left an imprint on me. I learned that living outside the box could get you in trouble, so I was determined to stay safe and small. Being agreeable provided me with safety and acceptance. Good girl conditioning meant I didn't want to add more to my parents' plate, so I became the kid who followed the rules. I channeled my writing talents into something that could be a "real" career (unlike my brother's slam poetry). Journalism allowed me to tell stories, but with rules and structure that felt sanctioned and safe.

It wasn't until I began unlearning the systems that taught me to shrink that I released the belief that I lack imagination. The Black feminists I spend time with always ask questions that expand my curiosity. "How would it feel to center care?" "How can we share the burden as a collective?" "Whose voice is missing?" There was also the time that a younger feminist challenged me to share what I want instead of what I don't.

Through community and discomfort, the edges of what I believed possible began to stretch. I still don't think of myself as naturally creative. I'm still not the first person in the room to cast a sweeping vision of the future or name the big idea. But I'm learning to ask the questions that tug at me, and explore the possibilities that feel just a hair out of reach. My brother always could, and I'm slowly finding my way there too.

Each time we ask "what if?", oppression loosens its grip. We gain a little distance from the box of acceptability many of us were trained to squeeze ourselves into. And with every expansion, curiosity returns as a practice that helps us imagine, question, and move toward something freer.

Workers Not Visionaries

Capitalism wants good workers, not people able to imagine a better world and willing to question why the system is built on extraction. The grooming begins early, with traditional education serving as training grounds. Schools teach that being good means following directions, coloring inside the lines, not being disruptive, and never questioning authority.

Imagination is dangerous because it asks questions about fairness, possibility, and who benefits and who pays. A system built on extraction can't afford people who imagine alternatives. Rocking the boat earns you labels like disruptive, immature, or unfocused, while those who toe the line are seen as responsible and mature. Compliance earns approval, and curiosity earns correction.

As always, it's not distributed evenly. Oppressive systems have denied certain people the right to explore, dream, invent, question, and imagine.

- Colonizers punished enslaved people for learning to read. Literacy fuels imagination, and imagination fuels rebellion.
- Men have told women and girls for centuries that their creative dreams are frivolous unless they serve someone else.
- The able-bodied world teaches disabled and neurodiverse folks that difference can get them disciplined, pathologized, institutionalized, or killed.
- Wealthy disparity pushes immigrants and working-class people into survival mode, where creativity is branded as impractical unless it turns a profit.
- The gender binary punishes and erases queer and trans folks for rejecting it because living outside it proves it was an invention in the first place.

This system teaches us early on to distrust our own questions and shrink our imaginative capacity. When people have the time, safety, and imagination to ask "Why?" or "What if?", they start to see the cracks in white-supremacist capitalist patriarchy, which is the last thing those in power want.

<table>
<tr><td rowspan="4">journal
your
journey</td><td>When did I learn that curiosity was dangerous?</td></tr>
<tr><td>Where in my life am I still coloring inside the lines?</td></tr>
<tr><td>What questions have I not allowed myself to ask?</td></tr>
<tr><td>What would I do differently if I trusted my curiosity?</td></tr>
</table>

Dreaming Is Radical

Visionary speculative fiction writer Octavia Butler understood that imagination is the real work of becoming your truest self. "Every story I create, creates me," she said. Butler warned that repressive societies have always understood the political danger of "wrong" ideas. If they can constrict what you believe is possible, they've already decided who you're allowed to become. Saidiya Hartman agrees and has said: "So much of the work of oppression is policing the imagination."

Policing imagination doesn't happen only through laws and violence. It happens through budgets, deadlines, metrics, and best practices. It shows up when ideas are filtered through profitability instead of possibility, and when creativity is allowed only after the "real work" is complete. Capitalism narrows imagination by making anything unprofitable feel irresponsible, indulgent, or naïve. Eventually, we stop asking expansive questions at all. Not because we lack imagination, but because we've learned it's not rewarded.

In *Freedom Dreams*, Robin D. G. Kelley reminds us that liberation movements have always started with dreamers. "Without new visions we don't know what to build, only what to knock down," he wrote. As Kelley's book highlights, the boldest dreamers have always been the most marginalized. If you're denied access, dignity, resources, and safety, then creating a better world is a matter of survival. Imagination becomes a lifeline when reality offers no refuge.

Toni Morrison once said that "oppressive language does more than represent violence; it is violence." The inverse is also true: liberatory imagination does more than inspire change; it creates it. Every movement began with people refusing to let the powerful define their possibilities. People who found each other in the margins, and whispered about a future not yet allowed.

And these movements began as theoretical blueprints long before they became policy or practice. Voting rights, marriage equality, the ADA ... these victories weren't realistic when first imagined. They became real because people were willing to hold visions larger than their circumstances, and to believe them possible even when there was no immediate proof.

Curiosity asks *"what if?"* and creativity gives shape to that more expansive future. Together, they help us see that we're capable of building something truer, kinder, and freer than anything we inherited. When we reclaim curiosity, we can see the cage. When we reclaim creativity, we can design the exit together.

"But I'm Not Creative"

Capitalism insists that only certain people are "creative," and it's usually those who turn it into a career or a revenue stream. What gets framed as "talent" is actually access, safety, time, and encouragement.

Creativity isn't a profession. It's a human instinct.

When your creativity gets starved out of you, it's not because you don't have it. It's because the system benefits when you forget you do. Creativity doesn't disappear; it goes underground, waiting for permission.

Permission Slip

I give myself unapologetic permission to make shit, try shit, and explore shit without needing it to be good or make money because my creativity matters.

X

Signature

The Power of 'What If?'

"What if?" is a subversive question. Oppression thrives on the status quo, and "what if?" cracks that wide open. It disrupts the myth of inevitability that white-supremacist capitalist patriarchy depends on. Every liberation movement began with a version of "What if we built something different?"

To practice "what if?" for your business, take time to journal:

- What if my business didn't run on urgency?
- What if work didn't require self-betrayal?
- What if the world could be arranged around care instead of extraction?
- What if rest, pleasure, and community were non-negotiable?
- What if I stopped asking for permission?

Ask "What if?" of yourself, your work, your relationships, your future. Ask it when you don't yet know the answer, and especially when the answer feels impossible. "What if?" is how new worlds begin.

Micro-Liberations

Reject the system that has tried to take curiosity and creativity from you.

Ask the forbidden question.
When something irritates you today, ask "Who does this actually serve?"
Write the answer down. Curiosity loosens the grip of inevitability.

Create without an audience.
Set a 10-minute timer and make something private: a note, doodle,
playlist, paragraph. Don't share it. Let creation exist without extraction.

Follow one spark.
When something delights you, confuses you, or pulls your attention,
follow it for five minutes with no agenda. Let wonder be enough.

Let yourself make something "bad."
Make something messy, incomplete, off-key, off-rhythm. Bad art is still
resistance, and it frees you from the obedience of perfection.

Play a little every day.
One moment of play a day (a dance break, silly voice, weird drawing)
interrupts the system's grip on your imagination.

Break one tiny rule.
Not the legally consequential kind, of course, but the polite, unspoken
ones meant to keep you small.

Your curiosity and creativity were never the problem. The system feared them because imagination is the first step toward liberation.

When you reclaim the parts of yourself that wonder, explore, question, and invent, you reclaim the power to write a future that isn't dictated by oppression. You learn to ask different questions, dream more boldly, and make choices that align with who you're becoming rather than who the world taught you to be. Curiosity is how every revolution begins. Creativity is how it continues.

If you do only one thing from this chapter, do this:
Ask yourself what curiosity has been asking for your attention,
and what would it take to give it five uninterrupted minutes?

<h1 style="text-align:center">22.</h1>

Collaboration as Rebellion

A few years into parenting, entrepreneurship, and pretending I could "do it all," I hit a wall. First came crying during a livestream in an online community when I admitted to myself that I didn't have friends. That moment cracked something in me, but it didn't fix the isolation.

Not long after, I read *Feminism Is for Everybody* by bell hooks. Reading about the consciousness-raising (CR) circles of the 1970s, I felt a sharp mix of grief and envy. It clicked that I didn't just want friends, I wanted community. I wanted my own CR circle to share truths, to witness one another, and to transform private troubles into political issues.

In the summer of 2019, I started an online feminist book club. I was desperate for conversation that wasn't about marketing funnels or nap schedules. I wanted to talk about justice and identity and power, and I wanted to do it with people who weren't afraid to admit they didn't have all the answers. I didn't monetize it. I just gathered a group of online friends to read liberation texts together, and share what they stirred up in us. When the world shut down in early 2020, the group became a lifeline. We were stuck at home, but we weren't alone in meaning-making or mutual care.

Once I experienced what real community could hold, I couldn't look back. What I thought was personal loneliness turned out to be a political condition. I remember the first time I co-created a workshop and how different it felt to build something *with* someone rather than *for* an audience. I shifted my solo business to partnerships with people who made the work fuller. The more I practiced collective care, the more I realized how much I'd been craving belonging (even if I couldn't name it).

That book club taught me that what we call loneliness is actually a collective wound, and that being held makes transformation possible. This chapter is about the kind of belonging that makes us brave enough to build something true.

Individualism Is a Scam

Settler colonialism framed land theft as discovery. The Protestant work ethic insisted that suffering was a sign of moral worth. By the time Herbert Hoover popularized "rugged individualism" in 1928, privileged Americans were already conditioned to believe that self-sufficiency was a marker of character and worthiness. Need was recast as weakness, dependence as failure, and survival as a solo achievement rather than something people had always done together.

The self-made myth, perfected by industrialists like Andrew Carnegie and repeated by nearly every billionaire since, omitted what wealth is actually built on—stolen land, exploited labor, inherited advantage, and unpaid care work. Those with the most privilege can afford to believe independence is noble because the structures around them do all the heavy lifting.

Not everyone was offered that story. For Black, Indigenous, immigrant, queer, and disabled people, collectivity has always been key to survival. Mutual aid, kinship networks, chosen family, and shared care are centuries-old practices built on the understanding that safety and liberation were never solo projects. Audre Lorde told us, "without community, there is no liberation." Isolation is where oppression does its quietest and most damaging work. Connection is how people live through what was designed to break them.

Dominant culture teaches the opposite lesson. Schools reward compliance and treat collaboration as cheating or weakness. Independence is framed as maturity. By adulthood, many of us, especially those socialized into privilege, have absorbed the belief that struggling alone is virtuous, and that needing others is something that healthy people outgrow.

We were never meant to do this alone. The belief that we were hasn't just isolated us, it's kept us focused on fixing ourselves instead of questioning what actually needs to change.

<table>
<tr><td rowspan="4">journal
your
journey</td><td>Where did I learn that I shouldn't need people?</td></tr>
<tr><td>What am I holding that doesn't belong to me alone?</td></tr>
<tr><td>How would community look if it centered care?</td></tr>
<tr><td>What do you need that you haven't yet admitted?</td></tr>
</table>

Community Is How We Get Free

Choosing community means reorganizing your life around a different logic than the oppressive norms. It's how we build futures we were never meant to imagine, let alone experience. It asks us to tolerate difference and discomfort. Community is slower, messier, and less predictable than going it alone, but it's also how we build durability instead of burnout. And that's only possible when we understand that our freedom is shared.

Audre Lorde said, "I am not free while any woman is unfree, even when her shackles are very different from my own." Collectivity is understanding that our struggles aren't identical, but our freedom is intertwined.

Mia Birdsong says in *How We Show Up* that belonging isn't something we stumble into, but something we practice. Liberatory community is built in small, consistent acts of showing up with truth instead of performance, curiosity instead of certainty, and care instead of comparison. In other words, community is a set of practices that change how decisions get made and who gets to shape them. It redistributes power in ordinary moments, not just in crises.

In business, that practice looks like:

- Building offers *with* your community, not *for* them.
- Creating feedback loops with people who have different lived experiences.
- Normalizing shared leadership vs. centering yourself.
- Sharing resources instead of gatekeeping them.
- Being transparent about money, time, and limitations.
- Redistributing visibility by spotlighting others' voices, especially those that are most underrecognized.
- Asking "Who else should be in this conversation?" before a decision.
- Making your invisible labor visible.

Disability justice leaders like Mia Mingus remind us that access isn't a favor or accommodation. It's a shared commitment. It's a way of saying, "Your freedom is tied to mine, and I will build with you." When we organize ourselves relationally instead of individually, access becomes culture.

Alone, our imaginations shrink to what we can personally carry. Together, we generate ideas no single person could hold alone. Collaboration deepens insight. Mutual care expands capacity. Shared risk builds courage. This is how liberation moves from theory into lived reality.

Unpacking Interdependence

*with **Erica Courdae,** a coach who helps executives take 'imperfect action' toward equity.*

Becky Mollenkamp: What is interdependence?

Erica Courdae: I deeply hate the self-made myth. You didn't do it all by yourself. You didn't hunt, fish, forage, build your house, sew your clothes, tend to your own medical care. Interdependence recognizes that you're not a lone ship in the night. Everything you do, and everything you have is tied to other people's labor, care, and presence.

Becky: What gets in the way of interdependence and collaboration?

Erica: We're conditioned to chase hyper-independence because we live under systems that actively punish interdependence. There are policies built specifically to keep us from feeding each other, housing each other, planting for each other, and depending on each other. That's not accidental. If we rely on each other, we rely less on the systems that profit from our isolation and our scarcity. To be in true community, we have to unlearn a lot of what capitalism and white supremacy taught us. Until then, we'll keep showing up to 'community' spaces as 50 little islands, each thinking, 'How do I get mine out of this?' instead of 'What can we build here together?'

Becky: Why does interdependence begin with self-exploration?

Erica: If you go into community without doing internal work, you drag your conditioning with you and replicate the harm you want to escape. Internal work is about clearing beliefs that break trust, so when you join community, you're not bringing a loaded weapon you didn't know you were holding.

Becky: How do we move from hyper-independence to interdependence?

Erica: It doesn't require you to become a different person. Start small. Look for where you tell yourself that you did it alone, or that you *should* do it alone. Where are you treating clients as transactions instead of relationships? Where are you hoarding knowledge or opportunities? Ask, 'Who have I been that I never consented to be?' That question can open big doors.

Audience	**vs.**	**Community**
Attention		Relationship
"Look at me"		"Let's look together"
Performance		Participation
Consumption		Contribution
Visibility		Witnessing
Transactional		Reciprocal
Scalable		Sustainable

If they don't know you, can't hold you, or won't challenge you, then you've created an audience, not a community.

Is Your Community Liberatory?

- ☐ People feel safe naming their needs.
- ☐ Power is shared, not hoarded.
- ☐ Access needs are named, honored, and integrated.
- ☐ Boundaries are respected without punishment or shame.
- ☐ Harm is addressed through repair, not silence or exile.
- ☐ People can show up imperfectly without fear of losing belonging.
- ☐ Joy, creativity, and play are part of the culture.
- ☐ Emotional labor is shared, not carried by the most marginalized.
- ☐ Transparency about decisions, money, and expectations is normalized.
- ☐ People speak *with* each other more than speaking *about* or *at* each other.
- ☐ No one is expected to ignore their body's needs to "keep up."
- ☐ Wisdom flows in multiple directions, not just top-down.
- ☐ The community asks: Who's missing? How do we create belonging?

Communities Every Entrepreneur Needs

Community isn't one thing. There are different circles for different needs:

- ***Nourishing community:*** People who hold you emotionally and remind you that you are more than your output. They invite you into laughter, play, and rest because they know that joy is fuel for resistance and renewal.
- ***Thinking community:*** People who challenge your ideas and help you decolonize your strategies. They ask questions you didn't consider, and remind you that your work can be bolder, deeper, and more aligned than you've let yourself consider.
- ***Doing community:*** People who collaborate, share resources, troubleshoot, and make the work lighter. These are the folks who jump into the weeds with you and understand that shared labor isn't charity.

Returning to Community

When you've been disappointed by past relationships, community can be intimidating. Here are small ways back in:

→ **Join as a witness first.** You don't have to arrive as your "best self." Listen. Observe. Let your nervous system acclimate.

→ **Start with low-stakes questions.** "What are you reading?" "What's bringing you joy?" Show curiosity as a first step toward building connection.

→ **Follow the warmth.** Notice who makes your body feel at ease and gets you excited to chat. Invest your energy with them.

→ **Show up consistently, not intensely.** One thoughtful interaction a week builds more community than a burst of enthusiasm followed by silence.

Making Decisions Collectively

Liberatory decisions account for power, impact, and responsibility. Here's a framework for making choices that don't recreate oppression:

Who is most impacted? → They lead.

Who has the least power? → They are centered.

Who has lived experience? → They guide.

Who has privilege? → They listen.

Who benefits and who is burdened? → Answer honestly, then adjust.

Micro-Liberations

Small ways to reclaim collectivism in a world that profits from your isolation.

Let someone help you.
Practice receiving without apology. Start small (a question, a long-delayed task) as a reminder that needs are invitations for connection.

Speak the truth out loud.
Tell one trusted person exactly what's hard right now—no fixing, no silver lining. Being witnessed is a form of care.

Practice "micro-delegation."
Hand off something small that you usually keep out of habit (scheduling, follow-up, formatting). Let someone else contribute to your ease.

Practice access intimacy.
Ask a friend today, "what do you need today to feel supported?" Then answer the question back so you can learn each other's access needs.

Initiate a small circle of care.
Choose two people and check in at the same time each week with one simple message: "Thinking of you. How are you *really*?"

Give without tracking the return.
Share a resource, make an intro, or pass along an opportunity without tracking reciprocity. Notice the relief of not keeping score.

We don't get free alone. Hyperindividualism is a story the system tells us so we won't realize how much stronger we become when we have each other.

When we gather, we remember our struggles aren't character flaws, they're systemic. When we collaborate, we remember we don't have to solve them alone. When we imagine collectively, we build futures no one could design alone.

Liberation is a group project. And the more we practice messy, mutual belonging, the more possible freedom becomes for all of us.

23.

Entrepreneurs as Activists

"For my first 15 years of entrepreneurship, I had a polished, careful, inoffensive version of myself I kept ready for business. I didn't hide my beliefs exactly, but I offered little more than lukewarm statements before slipping back into "professional mode." I was more afraid of alienating potential clients than I was committed to telling the truth.

Then the Supreme Court gutted Roe v. Wade. While I'd never been ashamed of my abortions, I'd felt my healthcare choices were separate from my business. With the dismantling of bodily autonomy, however, I understood the cost of my silence. That day, I told my subscribers about my abortions, then shared it on my blog and social media.

For the first time, my business felt aligned with my body instead of compartmentalized away from it. I no longer wanted to work with anyone who thought my healthcare, autonomy, or life were up for debate. There were consequences. A client asked for a refund. Hundreds of subscribers left my list. A few people sent angry emails. It stung. But the people who stayed (and those who have found me since) share my values, appreciate my candor, and would rather work with someone who tells the truth than someone who plays it safe. What I lost in reach, I gained in integrity. And my work immediately became easier to stand behind.

I used to think "professional" meant palatable, and keeping politics at a distance was a form of integrity rather than a form of fear. Thanks to my privilege, it took Dobbs for me to understand what many people never had the luxury of forgetting: that our work, bodies, and politics were never separate.

This chapter explores what it means to practice activism through everyday business choices—who you include, whose voices you elevate, and whose safety you protect. These aren't abstract questions. Every business answers them through its pricing, partnerships, speech, and silence.

Business is *Never* Apolitical

We're told that politics is a taboo topic, and that our silence on the issue makes us polite and professional. Only people with privilege can pretend politics are optional. Everyone else is already living inside the consequences.

White men invented professionalism in the late 19th and early 20th centuries as a gatekeeping mechanism to exclude women, Black people, immigrants, and disabled people from white male workplaces. It bans or punishes accents, natural hair, disability, gender nonconformity, anger, grief, and truth-telling. It decided who could be seen as credible, employable, and safe.

Making politics a matter of professionalism creates conformity. Workers who don't discuss wages won't unionize. Women who don't discuss harassment don't file complaints. Black and Brown people told not to talk about racism won't sue for discrimination. Breaking the silence brings consequences, which are not evenly distributed. Black, Brown, 2SLGBTQIA+, disabled, immigrant, and low-income people are punished far more harshly for naming injustice.

Entrepreneurs inherit this conditioning. We're told our livelihood depends on the "know, like, and trust" factor, so we need to be relatable (a coded way of saying "don't talk about politics"). As if our communities aren't impacted by racist policing, anti-trans laws, abortion bans, climate catastrophe, labor exploitation, and economic violence. As if business exists in a vacuum where people don't bring their identities, histories, and realities with them.

Pretending your politics don't exist requires erasing yourself in real time. It's exhausting, and deeply dehumanizing. And the parts of you that get erased are usually the ones that have survived the most. The truth is, everything is political. Pricing, hiring, marketing, and silence are political. Politics aren't the problem, oppression is. Naming it is the beginning of repair. Your business either challenges oppressive systems, or helps maintain them.

---

journal your journey

Where do I still cling to neutrality?

What am I afraid will happen if I name my politics?

How could my business become a site of solidarity?

How do my identities shape my responsibility to speak?

You Don't Need a Megaphone to Help

Your activism doesn't have to look like anyone else's. It just has to be aligned for you, grounded, and true to you. Deepa Iyer's *Social Change Ecosystem Map* is one of the clearest antidotes to the myth that activism is only marching and shouting from a megaphone. You might find yourself in one or more of these roles:

- Storyteller, shaping narratives that make systemic injustice visible.
- Weaver, connecting people who need to find one another.
- Builder, designing business structures that redistribute power and resources.
- Guide, helping clients understand the systemic forces shaping their choices.
- Caregiver, tending to emotional labor and community well-being.
- Disruptor, calling out harmful practices in your industry.
- Frontline Responder, mobilizing in moments of crisis.
- Visionary, imagining worlds beyond extraction, urgency, and domination.

None of these are more political than the others, and none are the real activist role. Movements require all of them, and most of us move between roles over time, responding to what our bodies and communities require. The work that sustains movements is often the least visible, and that doesn't make it any less radical or important.

Being political as an entrepreneur begins with naming the realities that shape your work (racism, capitalism, patriarchy, ableism, transphobia, classism) and refusing to pretend your business floats above them. It means aligning your actions with your values, even if it's quiet and imperfect.

You don't have to be the loudest or build a movement alone. You just have to take your place in the ecosystem in ways that honor your capacity, season, and privilege or oppression. Your business is already political through what it funds, normalizes, or ignores. It's up to you to decide if and how you participate with intention instead of avoidance.

You don't need to perform activism to practice it. Alignment that honors your capacity is more sustainable and more honest.

Making a Difference

Most activist work inside a business happens offline, in the everyday decisions about who and how we serve.

1. Restructure Your Business Around Your Values
- Make your pricing and payment plans ethical and transparent.
- Rewrite your policies to reflect care, not punishment.
- Build accessibility (captions, transcripts, pacing options) into every offer.
- Audit your business for urgency, extraction, or hierarchy, then revise.

2. Redistribute Power and Resources
- Redistribute a percentage of revenue to mutual aid.
- Share resources (signal boost, pass the mic) without expectation.
- Pay marginalized people for emotional, cultural, or educational labor.
- Offer community rates, sliding scales, or solidarity pricing as appropriate.

3. Shift How You Lead and Teach
- Name the systemic forces that shape your clients' experiences.
- Amplify others, especially marginalized leaders, without expectation.
- Make decisions that center the most impacted, not the most comfortable.
- Let community help shape your offers. Co-creation redistributes power.

4. Practice Repair and Accountability
- Name harm when it happens. Don't minimize, deflect, or rush resolution.
- Bake repair practices (how you'll address harm) into your policies.
- Examine your own privilege and responsibility.
- Seek feedback from those who experience your work differently.

5. Build in Collaboration, Not Competition
- Choose collaboration over competition whenever possible.
- Invite a colleague into your next project, brainstorm, or offering.
- Share tools, templates, and knowledge without scarcity.
- Let others be brilliant beside you. Their success doesn't diminish yours.

Micro-Liberations

Doable shifts to move your business toward true values alignment.

Name one system out loud.
Pick one place you show up (website, email footer, workshop intro) and name a system (racism, ableism, patriarchy) that shapes your industry.

Add a land acknowledgement.
Choose one place (homepage footer, event opening) to name the land you're on, and link to an Indigenous-led org that supports sovereignty.

Build accessibility into one offer.
Caption a video, add transcripts, offer asynchronous ways to participate. Accessibility is political; refusing to replicate ableist norms is the work.

Audit collaborations for equity.
Who are you platforming? Who gets paid? Who gets visibility? If the answers are uneven, adjust one thing before moving forward.

Publish clear boundaries.
Add a "No Tolerance for Hate" line to your site, community guidelines, onboarding doc. Name what happens if it shows up.

Add a repair sentence.
Outline your harm repair process. Add a line to offers: "Harm may happen here. If it does, we commit to naming and repairing it, and learning."

Deepa Iyer's ecosystem reminds us that no one carries a movement alone. We each have roles shaped by our gifts, capacity, and identities. When we act from the role that is ours, rather than the one we think we should perform, we become part of a collective force that is far stronger than individual effort.

Your job isn't to be everywhere or do everything, but to take your place in the ecosystem with clarity, courage, and care.

If you do only one thing from this chapter, do this:
Stop trying to be everything.
Locate your role in the ecosystem.
Take one concrete step this week that honors it.

24.

Taking Accountability

For most of my life, accountability felt like a personal attack. If someone called me in (or out), I'd feel defensive, rush to explain myself and prove that I was "actually a really nice person." Sometimes I cried. I almost always centered my feelings. In short, my behaviors were peak privilege.

Accountability felt like danger. I'd been taught that being perceived as good mattered more than being responsible. I grew up believing that voting "blue no matter who" and supporting liberal issues meant I was an ally. After reading bell hooks, Audre Lorde, and Angela Y. Davis, I understood how wrong I was. *White Feminism* by Koa Beck further helped me see that my need to be *seen* as good was getting in the way of actually *doing* good. It took years of unlearning for me to separate intent from impact, and to be called in without argument.

I'll never forget the moment where I knew I'd finally changed. I was running a group goal-planning call when a Black client shared that she wanted to lose weight. I launched into a lecture about the harms of diet culture. My intention didn't matter; the impact was a white woman instructing, or even scolding, the only Black woman about her body in a room full of white women. I caused harm, and I recognized it as it was happening.

After the call, I asked if she'd stay on to talk. I named exactly what I'd done without excuses, and apologized clearly and directly. Then I listened. She told me how it felt. I promised to learn from the moment and to change my behavior in the future. We left the conversation feeling more connected, not less, and I learned that accountability can deepen relationships.

I still feel defensiveness rise up sometimes. Privilege doesn't disappear because you read a few books or apologize well once. But I know now that harm is inevitable, and that repair is liberatory. I don't expect to stop causing harm. I expect myself to respond with integrity. This chapter is about moving from defensiveness to responsibility, and from individual guilt to collective repair.

181

The Politics of Repair

"Publicly owning up to a mistake and making an effort to do and be better is the best salve," Feminista Jones said in *Reclaiming Our Space*. But in business, accountability is deeply misunderstood, and frequently avoided. It's treated like damage control or punishment. In fact, accountability is how we stay in right relationship with ourselves and our communities.

The ability to avoid accountability is a privilege. Who gets the benefit of the doubt? Who gets excused as still learning? Who gets dragged? Who gets discarded? Who is allowed to grow? Who is denied the chance? The answers fall along predictable lines of race, gender, class, ability, and immigration status. The people with the least systemic power experience the greatest consequences. Meanwhile, those with the most privilege are often protected, forgiven, or even celebrated for taking responsibility for harm they caused.

Entrepreneurship culture only magnifies this imbalance. It teaches us to prioritize confidence over community, certainty over curiosity, and protecting our image over repairing our impact. "Expert energy" leaves no room for nuance. Capitalism piles on with its obsession with speed, scale, and perfection. In that landscape, harm is inevitable and repair is rare. When image matters more than relationship, accountability becomes impossible.

If your business interacts with human beings, accountability isn't optional. Your decisions ripple outward. Your policies shape people's experiences. Your silence has consequences, and your mistakes cause harm.

Liberatory business is not about getting it right all the time. That's impossible, and pretending otherwise just recreates the oppressive systems we're trying to dismantle. Building a liberatory business means accepting that harm will happen, and committing to repair (not defensiveness, hiding, and shame). Accountability isn't a threat to your credibility. It *is* your credibility.

journal your journey	How has privilege shaped how I feel re: being called in?
	Where do I rely on silence to avoid discomfort?
	Who holds me accountable with love and honesty?
	How might accountability look if I believed it was a gift?

From Harm to Healing

If you work with humans, you will cause harm. Not because you're a bad person, but because it's inevitable in relationships. Miscommunication happens. Power imbalances exist. Impact and intention don't always align. The question isn't whether you'll mess up, but if and how you'll repair it. Avoiding accountability doesn't prevent harm, it just transfers the cost to someone else. Repair is the difference between harm that heals and harm that festers.

Accountability isn't just for giant failures. Harm can come in everyday interactions, like changing plans without acknowledging the impact on others' time, making a decision without consulting those it affects, or thanking people privately while taking credit publicly. Unaddressed, these harms compound.

Barbara J. Love teaches that accountability is the fourth and final step of Liberatory Consciousness. It's looking at harm we cause, owning it fully, and changing course. Accountability is a practice of integrity, not a moral judgment. It can be uncomfortable, especially for those with the most privilege, until it becomes an embodied part of how you live and run your business.

Liberatory accountability is built on three pillars:

1. **Responsibility:** Name what happened without defensiveness or spin. Don't rewrite the story or center your feelings. Just tell the truth.
2. **Repair:** Ask, don't assume, what's needed. Understand that repair is a process, not a transactional apology.
3. **Reorientation:** Change systems, policies, and behaviors so the harm doesn't repeat. How will I behave differently? How will my structures behave differently? How will my community be safer because of this?

Accountability is shaped by power. The most marginalized people carry the biggest consequences for mistakes, while the most privileged are likely to be protected, praised, or forgiven. A liberatory approach flips that logic so that those with greater privilege bear greater responsibility to repair and change, and those who've been harmed aren't expected to educate, soothe, or mediate.

You don't have to collapse into shame when you mess up. As bell hooks said, "shame produces trauma, not change." This is about responsiveness, not perfection. Accountability asks you to stay curious and in relationship with the truth, even when it's uncomfortable (*especially* when it's uncomfortable). That's the path out of extraction and into integrity.

Accountability Across Privilege

Accountability isn't one-size-fits-all because it's shaped by power.

If you hold privilege, your job is to listen more, repair faster, and take critique without fragility. You have more protection in the world, which means you also carry more responsibility when harm happens.

If you hold marginalized identities, your job is not to absorb everyone else's harm. You don't owe education, soothing, or endless emotional labor. Your well-being matters, and boundaries are part of accountability too.

For everyone, context matters. Responsibility shifts depending on the room you're in, who's impacted, and where power sits.

5 Elements of a Liberatory Apology

1. **Name what happened clearly,** without euphemisms or softening.
2. **Acknowledge the impact,** not your intent or feelings.
3. **Name what you've learned**. Show understanding, not defensiveness.
4. **State what you'll do differently** (behavior, policy, or structural change).
5. **Follow through** because accountability without action is a performance.

When *Not* to Engage

→ You ***don't*** owe accountability to people who dehumanize you.

→ You ***don't*** owe education about your oppression.

→ You ***don't*** have to stay in a relationship to repair a harm you didn't cause.

Accountability is relational, not masochistic. If someone refuses to see your humanity, denies your lived experience, or demands emotional labor you don't have, stepping back isn't avoidance, it's protection. Boundaries are accountability to yourself, and that counts too.

***"We created a cult of unforgivability. Instead, we need to learn the power of forgiveness." Loretta Ross in* Calling In**

Micro-Liberations

Modest steps to strengthen your accountability muscles.

Name it first.
When you've caused harm, even small, acknowledge it. Don't wait for the person with less power to carry that labor.

Practice a no-excuses apology.
Issue an apology without padding, justification, or self-defense. "I'm sorry. I understand why this caused harm. Here's what I'm changing."

"Thank you for telling me."
Practice saying it out loud before responding to feedback. Notice how it slows defensiveness and signals safety.

Ask for consent before giving feedback.
Try: "Do you have capacity for feedback right now?" If the answer is no, honor it. Accountability without consent becomes control.

Write a "repair script."
When you're dysregulated, pause the conversation. "Thanks for naming this. I'm sorry. I need time to understand and will follow up by ______."

Close the loop.
If someone trusted you with feedback, follow up within 7 days with what changed. Repair that isn't reflected back is another broken promise.

Accountability won't always feel comfortable, especially for people socialized into privilege and conditioned to see being wrong as a threat to their moral goodness or authority. Avoidance leaves harm unaddressed. Accountability redistributes power, builds trust, and strengthens relationships.

Accountability isn't the absence of harm. It's the presence of repair. It's the understanding that to err is human, and to collectively heal is liberation.

25.

Legacy, Not Empire

When my fourth grade teacher asked us to share our life goals, I said, "I want to be in the encyclopedia someday." I wanted my life to matter, and even at nine, I'd learned that legacy meant being deemed important by institutions that were never built for me. What I didn't yet understand was that being important and being useful to each other aren't the same thing.

It wasn't until my life fell apart in my mid-30s (divorce, death, depression) that I asked myself what a meaningful life meant to *me*. The answer surprised me with its smallness. I wanted to help others live fuller, more honest lives. That became my work, and my work became my legacy. Every client who stops blaming themselves for systemic problems. Every entrepreneur who finds a way to run a business without replicating harm. Every community space that becomes a little more honest, spacious, or human. These small ripples feel more worthwhile than any encyclopedia entry ever could.

This book is part of my legacy, too. What you do with it also becomes part of my legacy, and part of yours. Every insight you remix, practice you adapt, or conversation you have becomes co-authorship. The ideas in these pages will travel into rooms I'll never enter, and shape decisions I'll never witness. The beauty of collective work is that its impact lives longer than any one person.

Motherhood made this undeniable. My son is my legacy not because he carries my DNA, but because he carries forward our shared values about moving through the world with care. The choices I make about how I show up for him ripple outward in ways I'll never see. And I'm someone's legacy, what the women who came before me made possible. None of us is the origin.

Legacy doesn't belong to us. What we build belongs to everyone it touches, and to all they go on to touch. It's greater than any encyclopedia entry. It's the quality of attention we bring to the people in front of us, passed forward by hands we'll never shake, into a world we'll never see.

Bigger Isn't Better (or Liberatory)

White-supremacist capitalist patriarchy sells entrepreneurs a very specific version of legacy. The goal is to scale until you dominate your market. If that sounds like empire building, it's because it is. Business borrows its definition of success directly from colonialism: expand, conquer, extract, control. Build something so big that it outlives you.

Access to resources, visibility, land, capital, and labor has always been distributed along predictable lines of race, class, gender, ability, and citizenship, which means empire building was never available to everyone. Empire rewards the already powerful, then tells the rest of us that if we can't build something massive, we're not thinking big enough or trying hard enough. Failure to dominate is reframed as a personal flaw instead of structural exclusion.

Even when the oppressed manage to gain access to resources, replicating empire building isn't liberatory. It only reshuffles who's positioned atop the hierarchy. Maintaining hierarchy with better intentions doesn't make it just. As Audre Lorde said, "the master's tools will never dismantle the master's house." Liberation can't be built with the same logic that created harm. Lorde again: "In our world, divide and conquer must become define and empower."

Empire-thinking seduces us with the illusion that dominance equals safety, permanence equals worth, bigness equals impact. But those metrics were designed to uphold hierarchy, not humanity. They teach us to measure success through accumulation rather than contribution, independence rather than interdependence, and control rather than connection.

The problem isn't who gets to build an empire. It's the logic that rewards domination in the first place. If we don't consciously reject it, we'll unconsciously recreate it. Real legacy is the communities strengthened by your presence and made steadier by your absence.

How do I want my business to make people feel?

Whose lives has my work already touched?

Whose flourishing do I want my work to support?

What am I building that others could inherit or expand?

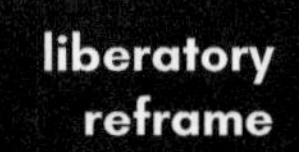

Making Space for Freedom

I once watched a founder cry in our first coaching session because her business had grown beyond anything she'd imagined, yet she felt like she couldn't take a day off without it unraveling. Empire logic centers everything on the founder, even when we don't want it to, because control is the point.

Empire asks: how long can this last? Liberation asks: who does this free? That's a big difference. If empire is about accumulation, permanence, and control, then liberatory legacy is about impact, redistribution, and collective care. Not what you build for yourself, but what you make possible for others.

This means designing for shared leadership, succession, and adaptation. It means letting others shape what you started instead of freezing it in your image. It means trusting that your work can evolve without your permission. Colonial logic says make something bigger than yourself. Liberatory logic says make something that doesn't depend on you.

Are you building a business that requires you to stay at the center forever? Or one that can thrive because you shared power, taught what you know, documented what you built, and opened doors for others?

Legacy isn't measured in size or name recognition. It's measured in care, redistribution, voices lifted, conditions changed, and opportunities passed forward. When we stop chasing empire, we start building interdependent, resilient, and nourishing ecosystems. Ecosystems don't crumble when a single leader leaves. They adapt and regenerate through collective stewardship.

"Your legacy is every life you've touched," Maya Angelou wrote. The future we're building is about communities capable of outliving any one founder. Not permanence for the powerful, but possibility for the many.

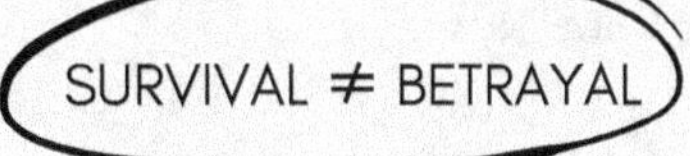

Being indispensable isn't a sign of success. It's a symptom of extraction. Legacy lives in what continues when you're no longer at the center. That's how work becomes bigger than any one person without becoming an empire.

Crafting a Business Legacy

Every entrepreneur's journey ends. Will you design it or default into it?

Traditional Sale
If you want to sell your business outright, keep the values intact by defining your non-negotiables: How must employees be treated? What practices must remain? Who cannot buy it?

Successor Leadership
Identify a team member, collaborator, or trusted partner who could take over when you're ready to step away, and start training them intentionally.

Cooperative or Collective Model
Transition ownership to the people doing the work through a worker co-op or shared-ownership model. This spreads power, wealth, and decision-making instead of consolidating it.

Community Stewardship Model
Your business becomes community-owned or community-guided, a living resource held by the people it serves.

Legacy Licensing
License your frameworks, tools, or systems, or make them open-source, so others can evolve them.

A Slow Sunset
Not every business needs to live forever. Some deserve a dignified, planned ending rather than an attempt at eternal growth.

Begin Building Your Plan Now
1. *Name your vision.* What do you want to last? What shouldn't last?
2. *Audit your power.* What knowledge and systems live in your head?
3. *Document everything* (systems, processes, values, rituals, relationships).
4. *Practice letting go.* Delegate, collaborate, redistribute decision-making.
5. *Pick a path.* Work toward an aligned exit (succession, co-op, sale).
6. *Revisit annually.* Let your plans evolve with you and your community.

Micro-Liberations

Small shifts to help move you toward the world you're trying to create.

Give credit publicly.
In your next email, post, or meeting, name a specific person or book that shaped your thinking and link to them. Don't generalize. Be concrete.

Make your lineage visible.
Add a short "Inspired by" line to your website that names the thinkers and communities that your work builds upon.

Make room on purpose.
Identify one meeting, project, or role you currently dominate and step back so someone else can lead it. Don't help. Make space and stay quiet.

Define success in community terms.
Choose one metric that reflects collective well-being (belonging, access, redistribution) and track it as seriously as you track revenue.

Preserve the wisdom of your mistakes.
Document one lesson you learned the hard way and what you'd do differently. Share it with a peer or community to save them the pain.

Build a succession-minded habit.
Ask, "What could continue without me?" Create a process so others can continue the work. Legacy starts when knowledge stops living in your head.

Legacy isn't built later. It's built in choices about how you lead, how you share power, how you redistribute resources, how you show care, how you tell the truth, and how you practice your politics when no one is watching.

Empire asks you to build something impressive. Liberation asks you to build something inheritable. Your legacy isn't your brand, audience, or revenue chart. It's every life you touch, every room you make safer, every person you leave better than you found them. That's the kind of legacy empire can't imagine.

Conclusion

The Slow Revolution

Entrepreneurs are sold the capitalist fairy tale that growth should be fast, and you're failing if you aren't working hard to make it happen. But every freedom movement worth its salt has taken generations, reminding us that real change is collective and slow. Movements aren't built at the pace of quarterly revenue targets, they're built at the pace of human beings healing, learning, unlearning, and choosing differently.

My own revolution has been slow. Slowly stripping away the identities I'd once used to prop myself up. Slowly grieving, rebuilding, and learning to trust myself again. Slowly unlearning the capitalist conditioning I thought was just how the world works. Slow like watching my brilliant, tired, over-functioning clients release the systems that have harmed them, and learn to honor their humanity. Their revolutions don't happen in a single breakthrough. They happen when they pause, renegotiate boundaries, and say "no" to make room for a deeper "yes." Sometimes that looks like a client deleting social media off their phone to make space for quiet. Sometimes it's a CEO admitting they can't keep doing 14-hour days and choosing rest. Sometimes it's someone finally letting themselves hire help.

Everything I care about (liberation, repair, relationship) is slow by choice and necessity. That wasn't always true, but choosing slow began to feel like choosing myself and a better future. And I could only get there once I realized that slowness isn't a failure of ambition, but a refusal of extraction.

Even now, I don't imagine myself as finished. Capitalism is the air we breathe. Even if you excavate it, you keep inhaling more. In a few years, I may look back at this book and see blind spots I can't yet name, lessons I've learned since writing it, places I'd want to completely change. That doesn't mean this work failed. It only means it's alive.

The relentless, punishing pace of capitalism isn't a flaw in the system. It *is* the system. Speed keeps us too exhausted, docile, and distracted to question anything. It convinces us that if change isn't immediate, it isn't real. It tells us we must choose between our humanity and our impact.

What's changed for me isn't that I've stopped breathing this air. It's that I can more quickly recognize it for what it is. Sometimes I can release it. Sometimes I can't. When I can't, I work with what's possible instead of pretending I'm above it. And I don't do that work alone anymore because I've cultivated a community of people equally invested in this work. That's the difference between knowing the system is harmful and having support while you learn how to live inside it without disappearing.

Slowness is how we reconnect with ourselves and each other. A slow revolution means intentionally refusing the urgency of systems that thrive on depletion. The slow revolution is not about waiting for the world to change. It's about changing the pace at which we move so we don't burn ourselves out before the world can meet us.

And here's the part that still catches in my throat: We likely won't see the full impact of our work in our lifetimes. Black feminists taught me that liberation work is generational work. As Audre Lorde said, "Revolution is not a one-time event." The entrepreneurs I coach, the communities I build, the pages of this book are contributions to a world I hope my son inherits, even though the transformation won't be complete by then (or even by the end of his lifetime). This is work we won't finish, but that we must refuse to abandon.

Revolution doesn't happen because a few people try to top the hierarchal ladder and shift where power lies. It happens because many of us choose to go steady and work collectively to knock down the ladder altogether.

If you've finished this book and don't plan to burn down your business or reinvent everything by next week, you understood the assignment. Liberation isn't a checklist, a blueprint, or a new set of rules to memorize. There's no tidy framework to download and implement between client calls. This is a lifelong practice rooted in curiosity, honesty, boundaries, repair, power-sharing, and the courage to stop performing and start belonging.

Liberation isn't pretending the cage never existed. It's recognizing when the door is open, and trusting yourself enough to step toward it. Sometimes that step is small or hesitant. Sometimes you pause at the threshold and return later. That doesn't mean you've failed. It means you're learning how freedom actually works.

If you take only one thing from this book, let it be this: You are not the problem. The system is. And you have more power to resist it and reshape what comes next than you've been led to believe. Every oppressive structure you've internalized was designed to make you doubt your own agency. When you stop believing the lies, the ground beneath them begins to crack.

The work ahead isn't about fixing yourself. It's about refusing to contort your humanity to fit a system built on extraction. It's about designing a business (and a life) that honors your capacity, community, values, and joy. It's about aligning your work with the world you want to help create, even if that world seems impossibly far away.

Here's your invitation: Keep going ... slowly, imperfectly, and collectively. Let this book be a beginning, not a destination—and definitely not a standard you feel you must compare yourself to. Let it crack something open in you, perhaps a truth you can't unsee or a permission you didn't know you needed. Then put it into practice. One choice, conversation, boundary, or collaboration at a time. Not perfectly or permanently. Just honestly, again and again and again. And when you feel yourself slipping back into old patterns, pause, breathe, call in your community, and begin again.

Your slow revolution starts wherever you are. It's not about waiting until you feel ready or for the world to no longer be on fire. It starts now, in the messy middle of real life with its bills, obligations, and grief.

If that feels scary, remember that you're not doing this alone. You're part of a lineage of people who have always imagined freer worlds and planted seeds they knew they'd never see grow. You're part of a community of entrepreneurs choosing equity over ego, interdependence over individualism, and liberation over the illusion of control. You're held by others who refuse to abandon their humanity, even when the systems around them demand it. As my most powerful teacher, bell hooks, said: "Rarely, if ever, are any of us healed in isolation. Healing is an act of communion."

Together, we get to decide what the future of work looks like. We get to practice a new way of being. **Together, we get free.**

Acknowledgements

This book is a collective effort. It wouldn't exist without the people whose generous education shaped my thinking, nor without the friends, family, and business collaborators who provided the spaciousness and encouragement I needed to finish it. Writing often feels solitary, but the truth is this book was sustained by communal care.

I'm indebted to my fellow feminists, both those I know personally and those I'll never meet. I'm especially grateful to the Black thinkers, disability justice activists, Indigenous teachers, and movement builders who've spent generations naming how power operates and imagining how we create something just and equitable. This book is in conversation with your work. You didn't just inform my thinking, you've changed how I live.

There aren't enough thanks to give to my brilliant business partners, Taina Brown and Faith Clarke. They've been my greatest teachers, kept things running when I fell behind, and became my greatest cheerleaders when I wanted to quit writing. They've shown me what leadership looks like when power circulates.

I'm also deeply grateful to my clients for trusting me with their stories. They've taught me as much about care, boundaries, leadership, and liberation as any business book ever has. Watching you choose yourselves and your communities has been one of the great honors of my life.

Thanks also to the communities that have held me, challenged me, and practiced liberation alongside me in real time. The Feminist Podcasters Collective and the Messy Liberation Coaches Circle are living proof that community is not "nice to have," but necessary for survival and joy. And to the dozens of women in the mastermind groups I've been part of over the last decade, thank you for helping me dream bigger.

Thank you to the people who generously gave their time, insight, and care by offering feedback on this book and helping shepherd it into the world. Your advice and reflections strengthened this work. And to the launch team, your willingness to talk about, recommend, and share this book was an act of trust and solidarity.

My friends and family held me when grief tried to consume me, reminded me who I am when I forgot, and loved me for who I am (not what I do). Mom, thank you for modeling strength, care, intelligence, and fortitude. Lindsey, thank you for seeing the best in me when I was at my absolute worst. Terry, it was always you (and it always will be). How did I get so lucky? And to my sweet, smart, funny, empathetic, and handsome Gus, thank you for being you. Every day you show me what's possible when we let our hearts guide us. You're my daily reminder that a better world is worth fighting for, and I can't wait to watch you step even further into your greatness.

Finally, thank *you* for being here. I'm grateful for every reader willing to question the rules we've been handed, and to imagine with me something more humane. If this book helped you feel less alone, more resourced, or even a little braver about choosing yourself, then it has already done its job.

This work grows in community. I'm grateful you're part of it.

References

Introduction

Angelou, Maya. *I Know Why The Caged Bird Sings*. Random House, 1969.

Crenshaw, Kimberlé. *Mapping the Margins: Intersectionality, Identity Politics, and Violence against Women of Color*. Stanford Law Review, Vol. 43, No. 6, July 1991.

hooks, bell. *Feminism Is for Everybody*. South End Press, 2000.

hooks, bell. *All About Love: New Visions*. HarperCollins, 1999.

Chapter 1

Lebron, Trudi. *The AntiRacist Business Book: An Equity Centered Approach to Work, Wealth, and Leadership*. Row House Publishing, 2022.

Love, Dr. Barbara J. *Developing a Liberatory Consciousness*. In M. Adams, W. J. Blumenfeld, C. R. Casteneda, H. W. Hackman, M. L. Peters, and X. Zuniga (Eds.), *Readings for Diversity and Social Justice* (pp. 533-540). Routledge, 2010.

Chapter 2

Oluo, Ijeoma. *So You Want to Talk About Race*. Seal Press, 2018.

Vaid-Menon, Alok. *Beyond the Gender Binary*. Penguin Random House, 2020.

Scruggs-Hussein, Tovi. https://www.ticiess.com/

hooks, bell, *Outlaw Culture: Resisting Representations*. Routledge, 2006.

Menakem, Resmaa. *My Grandmother's Hands*. Central Recovery Press, 2017.

Kimmerer, Robin Wall. *Braiding Sweetgrass: Indigenous Wisdom, Scientific Knowledge and the Teachings of Plants*. Milkweed Editions, 2013.

Chapter 3

Martin, Dr. Raquel. https://www.raquelmartinphd.com/

Brown, Taina. https://www.ifthenand.org/

Chapter 4

Bonilla-Silva, Eduardo. *Racism Without Racists: Color-Blind Racism and the Persistence of Racial Inequality in America*, Rowman and Littlefield Publishers, 2003.

Shakur, Assata. *Assata: An Autobiography*. Lawrence Hill Books, 2001.

Birdsong, Mia. *How We Show Up: Reclaiming Family, Friendship, and Community*. Grand Central Publishing, 2020.

Chapter 5

Hersey, Tricia. *Rest is Resistance: A Manifesto*. Little, Brown, and Company, 2022.

Lorde, Audre. *Sister Outsider: Essays and Speeches*. The Crossing Press, 1984.

Kaba, Mariame. *We Do This 'Til We Free Us: Abolitionist Organizing and Transforming Justice*. Haymarket Books, 2021.

Kimmerer, Robin Wall. *The Serviceberry: Abundance and Reciprocity in the Natural World*. Scribner, 2024.

Kimmerer, Robin Wall. *Braiding Sweetgrass: Indigenous Wisdom, Scientific Knowledge and the Teachings of Plants*. Milkweed Editions, 2013.

brown, adrienne maree. *Emergent Strategy: Shaping Change, Changing Worlds*. AK Press, 2017.

Cargle, Rachel. https://rachelcargle.com/

Chapter 6

Kimmerer, Robin Wall. *The Serviceberry: Abundance and Reciprocity in the Natural World*. Scribner, 2024.

Kimmerer, Robin Wall. *Braiding Sweetgrass: Indigenous Wisdom, Scientific Knowledge and the Teachings of Plants*. Milkweed Editions, 2013.

Timmons, Jacquette. https://www.jacquettetimmons.com/

Chapter 7

Suzman, James. *Work: A Deep History, from the Stone Age to the Age of Robots*. Penguin Press, 2021.

Hartman, Saidiya. https://saidiyahartman.com/

brown, adrienne maree. *Emergent Strategy: Shaping Change, Changing Worlds*. AK Press, 2017.

Smith, Toi. https://www.toimarie.com/

Chapter 8

Ajayi Jones, Luvvie. *Professional Troublemaker: The Fear-Fighter Manual*, Penguin Random House, 2021.

brown, adrienne maree. *Emergent Strategy: Shaping Change, Changing Worlds*. AK Press, 2017.

Chapter 9

Hersey, Tricia. *Rest is Resistance: A Manifesto*. Little, Brown, and Company, 2022.

Kendall, Mikki. *Hood Feminism: Notes from the Women That a Movement Forgot*. Viking, 2020.

hooks, bell. *All About Love: New Visions*. HarperCollins, 1999.

Love, Dr. Barbara J. *Developing a Liberatory Consciousness*. In M. Adams, W. J. Blumenfeld, C. R. Casteneda, H. W. Hackman, M. L. Peters, and X. Zuniga (Eds.), *Readings for Diversity and Social Justice* (pp. 533-540). Routledge, 2010.

Freire, Paulo. *Pedagogy of the Oppressed*. Continuum, 1970.

Chapter 10

Hersey, Tricia. *Rest is Resistance: A Manifesto*. Little, Brown, and Company, 2022.

Federici, Silvia. *Caliban and the Witch: Women, the Body and Primitive Accumulation*. Autonomedia, 2004.

Kimmerer, Robin Wall. *Braiding Sweetgrass: Indigenous Wisdom, Scientific Knowledge and the Teachings of Plants*. Milkweed Editions, 2013.

Stephens, Desireé B. https://desireebstephens.com/

Chapter 11

Hari, Johann. *Stolen Focus: Why You Can't Pay Attention and How to Think Deeply Again*. Crown, 2023.

Zuboff, Shoshana. *The Age of Surveillance Capitalism: The Fight for a Human Future*. Public Affairs, 2019.

Noble, Safiya. *Algorithms of Oppression How Search Engines Reinforce Racism*. NYU Press, 2018.

Hruby, Amelia. *Your Attention is Sacred: Except on Social Media*. 2025.

Chapter 12

Lebron, Trudi. *The AntiRacist Business Book: An Equity Centered Approach to Work, Wealth, and Leadership*. Row House Publishing, 2022.

Thompson, Sonia. https://www.frictionlessgrowthlab.com/

Adaway, Desiree. https://adawaygroup.com/

Diels, Kelly. https://kellydiels.com/

Chapter 13

Noble, Safiya. *Algorithms of Oppression How Search Engines Reinforce Racism*. NYU Press, 2018.

Nwangwu, N. Chloé. https://www.nobiworks.com/

Rodriguez, Stefanie O'Connell. https://tooambitious.com/

Chapter 14

Hines, Ericka. https://www.blackwomenthriving.com/

Crenshaw, Kimberlé. *Mapping the Margins: Intersectionality, Identity Politics, and Violence against Women of Color*. Stanford Law Review, Vol. 43, No. 6, July 1991.

Chapter 15

Collins, Patricia Hill. *Black Feminist Thought: Knowledge, Consciousness, and the Politics of Empowerment*. Routledge, 1990.

Brown, Taina. https://www.ifthenand.org/

Interlude: After I Couldn't Unsee It

Armbrust, Jennifer. *Proposals for the Feminine Economy*. The Fourth Wave, Topanga, 2018.

Harquail, CV. *Feminism: A Key Idea in Business*. Routledge, 2019.

Chapter 16

Cottom, Tressie McMillan. https://tressiemc.com/

Lebron, Trudi. *The AntiRacist Business Book: An Equity Centered Approach to Work, Wealth, and Leadership*. Row House Publishing, 2022.

Chapter 17

Lebron, Trudi. The AntiRacist Business Book: An Equity Centered Approach to Work, Wealth, and Leadership. Row House Publishing, 2022.

Opie, Dr. Tina and Dr. Beth A. Livingston. Shared Sisterhood: How to Take Collective Action for Racial and Gender Equity at Work. Harvard Business Review Press, 2022.

Clarke, Faith. https://faithclarke.com/

Chapter 18

brown, adrienne maree. *Emergent Strategy: Shaping Change, Changing Worlds*. AK Press, 2017.

Eltahawy, Mona. *The Seven Necessary Sins for Women and Girls*. Beacon Press, 2019.

Love, Dr. Barbara J. *Developing a Liberatory Consciousness*. In M. Adams, W. J. Blumenfeld, C. R. Casteneda, H. W. Hackman, M. L. Peters, and X. Zuniga (Eds.), *Readings for Diversity and Social Justice* (pp. 533-540). Routledge, 2010.

Chapter 19

Hemphill, Prentis. *What it Takes to Heal: How Transforming Ourselves Can Change the World*. Random House Publishing Group, 2024.

Chapter 20

Hochschild, Arlie. *The Second Shift: Working Families and the Revolution at Home*. Viking, 1989.

Hersey, Tricia. *Rest is Resistance: A Manifesto*. Little, Brown, and Company, 2022.

brown, adrienne maree. *Pleasure Activism: The Politics of Feeling Good*. AK Press, 2019.

Maney, Jordan. https://www.jordanmaney.com/

Chapter 21

Butler, Octavia. https://www.octaviabutler.com/

Hartman, Saidiya. https://saidiyahartman.com/

Kelley, Robin D. G. *Freedom Dreams: the Black Radical Imagination*. Beacon Press, 2002.

Morrison, Toni. https://www.tonimorrisonsociety.org/

Chapter 22

hooks, bell. *Feminism is for Everybody: Passionate Politics*. Routledge, 2014.

Lorde, Audre. *Sister Outsider: Essays and Speeches*. The Crossing Press, 1984.

Birdsong, Mia. *How We Show Up: Reclaiming Family, Friendship, and Community*. Grand Central Publishing, 2020.

Mingus, Mia. https://leavingevidence.wordpress.com/

Chapter 23

Iyer, Deepa. *Social Change Now: A Guide for Reflection and Connection*. Skinner House Books, 2024.

Chapter 24

Beck, Koa. *White Feminism: From the Suffragettes to Influencers and Who They Leave Behind*. Atria Books, 2021.

Jones, Feminista. *Reclaiming Our Space: How Black Feminists Are Changing the World from the Tweets to the Streets*. Beacon Press, 2019.

Love, Dr. Barbara J. Developing a Liberatory Consciousness. In M. Adams, W. J. Blumenfeld, C. R. Casteneda, H. W. Hackman, M. L. Peters, and X. Zuniga (Eds.), Readings for Diversity and Social Justice (pp. 533-540). Routledge, 2010.

Ross, Loretta. *Calling In*. Simon and Schuster, 2025

Chapter 25

Lorde, Audre. Sister Outsider: Essays and Speeches. The Crossing Press, 1984.

About the Author

Becky Mollenkamp is a feminist business coach for service-based entrepreneurs who want to build human-first businesses that honor collective flourishing over profit-at-all-costs growth.

Her work didn't begin in coaching. Becky holds a master's degree in communications and, for nearly 20 years, she worked in journalism, first at a daily newspaper, then at *Better Homes and Gardens,* and later as a freelance writer and editor, before she eventually moved into content marketing for corporate clients. She spent a decade working inside the very systems she'd eventually question.

Becky shifted to coaching more than a decade ago. Over the years, her work has been transformed by Black feminist thought, disability justice, and abolitionist frameworks. Through one-on-one coaching, podcasting, writing, and collective spaces, she now supports her entrepreneur clients in redefining success outside of white-supremacist capitalist patriarchal conditioning.

In addition to coaching, Becky co-runs Feminist Founders with Faith Clarke and the Messy Liberation Coaches Circle with Taina Brown. She also founded and runs the Feminist Podcasters Collective.

Becky lives in St. Louis, Missouri with her husband and son.

www.ingramcontent.com/pod-product-compliance
Lightning Source LLC
Chambersburg PA
CBHW071508140726
47997CB00005B/1901